ONCE
UPON
A
MYSTERY

What Happens Next?

MICHAEL E. MOYNAHAN, S.J.

PAULIST PRESS
New York/Mahwah, N.J.

Library of Congress Cataloging-in-Publication Data

Moynahan, Michael E.
  Once upon a mystery : what happens next? / by Michael
E. Moynahan.
       p.   cm.
  ISBN 0-8091-3791-7 (alk. paper)
  1. Bible plays, American. 2. Bible. N.T. Gospels—Study and teaching. 3. Drama in Christian education. 4. Catholic Church—Education. 5. Bible. N.T. Gospels—Liturgical use. 6. Drama in public worship. 7. Catholic Church—Liturgy. I. Title.
BV1534.4.M685   1998
246'.72—dc21   98-23004
                                                        CIP

Cover design and interior artwork by Bruce Crilly

Book design by Mark Scala

Published by Paulist Press
997 Macarthur Boulevard
Mahwah, New Jersey 07430

Printed and bound in the
United States of America

Contents

This book is dedicated to
Pablo and Consuelo Prietto,
Ercelia McGuire,
Aloysius Valentine Moynahan
and Helen Moynahan:
five stories of God's presence
and love in my life.
The witness of their lives
has given me a glimpse
of what happens next.

Introduction

I remember, as a child growing up in the 50's, going to the Fox movie theater in downtown Phoenix, Arizona, almost every Saturday morning. Besides the "live" entertainment, the cartoons and feature film, we were always treated to another installment of an adventure serial. From week to week we were engulfed in mystery. We would not know what was going to happen to the heroine tied to the railroad tracks with that speeding locomotive about to crush her, or to the hero lying unconscious in the cavernous hideout of villains who had left him to be destroyed by the planted explosives that were about to go off. Each Saturday I joined hundreds of other children in wondering what would happen next week.

Gospel parables and miracle stories are filled with mystery. They leave us dangling, wondering and imaginatively engaged. There are so many "unanswered questions" in the gospels that engage us and transform us, if we let them. For instance, what happened to the magi when they returned home? (Mt 2:1-12) How did the centurion's life change after Jesus healed his servant? (Mt 7:5-13) How did the multiplication of the loaves and fishes influence the five thousand or more people who experienced this event in the desert? (Mt 14:13-21) Whatever became of the paralytic who was brought to Jesus by four friends? (Mk 2:1-12) What happened to the demoniac from the country of the Gerasenes after he was healed by Jesus and sent back to his people? (Mk 5:1-20) What became of Bartimaeus, the blind beggar, who recovered his sight and followed Jesus "on the way"? (Mk 10:46-52) Did the victim in the parable of the Good Samaritan live or die? If he lived, did his opinion of foreigners (i.e. Samaritans) change as a result of being helped by one? (Lk 10:25-37) In the parable of the prodigal child, did the parent

1

succeed or fail in reconciling his two children? (Lk 15:11-32) How was Zacchaeus' life changed as a result of his encounter with Jesus? (Lk 19:1-10) What happened to the Samaritan woman as a result of her encounter with Jesus at the well? (Jn 4:1-42) What became of the man born blind after he was healed by Jesus and expelled from the synagogue by the religious leaders? (Jn 9:1-41) What happened to Lazarus after being raised from the dead? (Jn 11:1-44) As you can see, the gospels are full of stories that invite our engagement by asking us to imagine: "What happened next?"

The biblical dramas in this volume are divided into five parts. First, there is the *scriptural passage* that inspires, shapes and colors everything after it. Second, there is the *biblical drama* which represents the attempt of one faith community to make some imaginative connections between the realities of the scriptural story and the realities of the faith community's life. Third, there is a list of *props* that were used in the original performance of the drama. Fourth, there are some *production notes* that explain the influences that shaped the creation of each biblical drama. Fifth, there are some *reflection questions and exercises* that invite extended imaginative engagement with both the scriptural passages and the biblical dramas to uncover more of the faith and wisdom in them that can assist and encourage spiritual pilgrims in their faith journey.

Santa Clara University is currently on an academic quarter system. The Biblical Explorers were a group of students who volunteered to work with me each quarter. The Explorers would take a gospel passage each quarter and creatively work with it. The result was a dramatic interpretation of this piece of scripture which served as the homily on the given Sunday. Since the Explorers spent six or seven weeks working with a particular passage, this meant that they usually worked with scriptures from the latter part of each quarter.

The human experiences captured in each drama's vignettes are clearly those of university students. They can, however, have broader appeal and application. I suggest that you use those vignettes which your study group or liturgy group feel best capture their community's experiences and challenges. Remember to adapt wherever and whenever possible. These dramas come out of the attempt to discover connections between the reality of the word of God and the reality of the experience of a particular faith community.

A Quaker student once told me that during Quaker meetings, when one person speaks in such a way that others experience his/her words as true, they say: "That friend speaks to my experience." If these vignettes speak to some of the experiences of your faith community, use them. If they don't quite capture your faith community's experience, adapt them or use them as models to create some short dramatic vignettes of your own.

The number of roles in each drama reflects the number of participants in the Biblical Explorers' process that quarter. You can have your group take multiple roles if you don't have as many people as a particular drama requires. There is nothing mysterious about the names used in the dramas. They are the names of the Biblical Explorers involved in creating that particular drama. I strongly suggest that you use only one or two of the vignettes from a particular drama for your worship or study purposes. Otherwise, the biblical drama can become too long and draw undue attention to itself. Nothing is used effectively in liturgy when it diverts attention to itself rather than supporting the action of liturgy.

There are some features of the biblical dramas in *Once Upon a Mystery: What Happens Next?* that were begun in *Once Upon a Miracle* (Mahwah, NJ: Paulist Press, 1990) and have found a more extensive development in this collection. The first feature is that aspects of Ignatian Spirituality, based on the *Spiritual Exercises* of St. Ignatius of Loyola, have found a more prominent place in the reflection questions and exercises. My Jesuit background and the development of a course on Ignatian Spirituality, which I taught to third and fourth year university students, are responsible for this.

The second feature is the pronounced presence of questions about the relationship of "faith" and "actions for justice." There are four contributing influences to this. The first influence was the wonderful way that the university students who comprised the Biblical Explorers were endeavoring to integrate their own faith with their concern and action for justice. They continually proposed challenging questions about what an authentic Christian response would be to the events unfolding around them. The second influence was extended conversations and exposure to the catechetical work of Sr. Anne Marie Mongoven, O.P., which made me increasingly aware of the critical place of "actions for justice" in the life and worship of the faith community. That awareness was sharpened by my own reading, reflecting and conversations on the necessity of "action for justice" in any authentic Christian catechetical or liturgical gathering. The third influence was the experience of injustice in our university, our Church, our city, our state, our country, and our world. Invariably, as we wrestled with the connection between the scriptures and our lived experience, we confronted the consistency or inconsistency of our supposed Christian values and our sometimes ambivalent behaviors. The fourth influence was the death of six Jesuits, their cook and her daughter, at the University of Central America. This event profoundly influenced many and shocked this Jesuit into a realization and consideration of all those other people in El Salvador, Central America, the Middle East, and throughout the world whose deaths lit a light that will never be extinguished. The courageous example of laying down their lives so that others might finally experience justice challenges each of us who call ourselves Christian to ask the triple questions that St. Ignatius proposes for retreatants in the *Spiritual Exercises:* "What have I done for the Christ who is suffering in the voiceless and the powerless?" "What am I doing for the Christ who is suffering in the voiceless and the powerless?" "What ought I to do for the Christ who is suffering in the voiceless and the powerless?"

How can you use the material in *Once Upon a Mystery: What Happens Next?* The dramas, with their reflection questions and exercises, can be used by all spiritual pilgrims. They can be used for times of prayer and retreat. They can be used by teachers who are trying to help students grow in the awareness, experience and expression of their faith. Scripture was meant to be studied in community. It is a treasure that belongs to the community. The dramas and reflection questions and exercises invite that type of imaginative engagement and "faith sharing" that will promote communal and individual faith development. Finally, these biblical dramas and reflection questions and exercises may assist all those who proclaim God's word or offer scriptural reflections in a liturgical setting.

I would like to acknowledge the invaluable contribution of the Biblical Explorers of Santa Clara University who contributed to the exploration and creation of these dramas. When I remember and give thanks for the blessings of my years at Santa Clara University, those blessings all have names like: Brian Ching, Anne Ensminger, Mark Lang, Krista and Ed Hochstatter, Christi Montes-Gotwald, Cari Zieske, David Giammona, Pam Romano, Craig De Poole, Jenny Girard, Chris Fowler, Garth Ashbeck, Ignacio Osorio, Tarie Regan, Paul Lampe, Peter Lampe, Chris Buchanan, Kristie Schindele, Ron Andre, Nancy Nissan, Dan Anderson, Maria McGill, Bro. Ben Foy, Laura Bertone, Christie Haddad, Harry Dimijian, Therese Inkmann, Tom Ligda, Kelly Gawrych, Alvaro Orozco, Lelanya Black, Marco Campagna, Jennifer

Cummins, Paul Leonard, Nicole Mayer, Eileen Minor, Jeff McCabe, Jen Elmore, O. J. Solander, Maureen Meagher, Ryan Kelsey, Eileen Agbay, Michelle Anselmo, Michael Thanos, Amy Harris, Jennine Lennox, etc., etc.. Your name is legion! I have and will continue to give thanks to God whenever I think of you. I hope each of you continues to grow in the desire and the ability to make those connections between faith and life.

From the time I went to Santa Clara University in 1985 and began the Biblical Explorers, I was constantly encouraged and supported in this work by Sr. Maureen Schaukowitch, OSF, Director of Campus Ministry, and her entire staff. During those eleven years a few members of the Campus Ministry staff participated in the Biblical Explorers. I remember with great gratitude the presence and participation of Krysha Cox-Harrington and Rosemary O'Brien-Wilson.

There were times when some members of the Religious Studies Department found this imaginative work of mine questionable and a distraction from the work of "serious scholarship." Maureen and her staff always found ways to remind me of the importance and place of the pastoral theology that these dramas represent. Campus Ministry supported this exploration of our biblical faith through the creation of these biblical dramas. The nine biblical dramas that appear in this book reveal the interpretive connections that Biblical Explorers discovered between the questions of the particular scriptural story and the questions of our life, between the challenges of the particular scriptural story and the challenges of our life lived in faith, between the realities of the particular scriptural story and the realities of our life. These biblical dramas, reflection questions and exercises represent, in imaginative form, what is at the heart of pastoral theology: giving shape to the community's faith and making it available to others in ways that shed light on the presence of God in all of life.

I am also deeply grateful to the Jesuit Community at Santa Clara University for the past eleven years. Tenny Wright, a true "soul friend," was ruthlessly honest in his feedback regardless of whether he liked or disliked a particular drama. Bob Senkewicz, Steve Privett, Jim Reites and Tom Shanks continually offered me both encouragement and helpful advice that shaped a current or future drama. I am particularly grateful to Jerry McKevitt, the religious Superior, and the entire Jesuit Community of Santa Clara University who provided me with a sabbatical for this writing project. Without all of their generous time and support *Once*

Upon a Mystery: What Happens Next? would not have been started or completed.

Additional thanks go to the Jesuit Community at Farm Street in London, England, for their hospitality as well as providing me with an environment that stimulated me to see this work through to completion. I was fortunate enough to have two Jesuits in London whose enlightening conversations often sparked further reflection for me on these biblical dramas as well as study questions and exercises. I am grateful to Richard Leonard of the Australian Province and Bill Broderick of the English Province for their companionship and lively interactions during my sabbatical.

Larry Boadt of Paulist Press has been a faithful and extremely supportive editor. I continue to be grateful for all the encouragement and support he has given to this manuscript as well as previous projects. John Mossi, a classmate and close friend in the Society of Jesus, made many creative suggestions that improved the sense and readability of this manuscript.

Once Upon a Mystery: What Happens Next? could be the title of the latest chapter of my own faith journey. After working at Santa Clara University since 1985, I moved to Gonzaga University in Spokane, Washington, to begin work as Associate Director of Continuing Education and Renewal Programs. With that gift of a small sabbatical to complete this writing project, I will hopefully know a little bit more about what the participants in the *Credo/Focus* program are experiencing during their sabbatical year and consequently be a wiser and more helpful companion to them on their journey.

While these biblical dramas will not replace the original stories they are intended to interpret, they hopefully will help you and your study groups to imaginatively engage the scriptures long enough to be changed by them. May the scriptural stories themselves, these biblical dramas, the reflection questions and exercises that follow each drama, and all the other forms of imaginative engagement that suggest themselves to you from these pages continue to help you and your faith community discover and express the life-giving *connections* between the realities of the scriptures and the realities of your life.

Michael E. Moynahan, S.J.
Gonzaga University
Spokane, WA 99258

1. The Prodigal Child

(Luke 15:11-32)

And he said, "There was a man who had two sons; and the younger of them said to his father, 'Father, give me the share of property that falls to me.' And he divided his living between them. Not many days later, the younger son gathered all he had and took his journey into a far country, and there he squandered his property in loose living. And when he had spent everything, a great famine arose in that country, and he began to be in want. So he went and joined himself to one of the citizens of that country, who sent him into his fields to feed swine. And he would gladly have fed on the pods that the swine ate; and no one gave him anything. But when he came to himself he said, 'How many of my father's hired servants have bread enough and to spare, but I perish here with hunger! I will arise and go to my father, and I will say to him, "Father, I have sinned against heaven and before you; I am no longer worthy to be called your son; treat me as one of your hired servants."' And then he arose and came to his father. But while he was yet at a distance, his father saw him and had compassion, and ran and embraced him and kissed him. And the son said to him, 'Father, I have sinned against heaven and before you; I am no longer worthy to be called your son.' But the father said to his servants, 'Bring quickly the best robe, and put it on him; and put a ring on his hand, and shoes on his feet; and bring the fatted calf and kill it, and let us eat and make merry; for this my son was dead, and is alive again; he was lost, and is found.' And they began to make merry. Now his elder son was in the field; and as he came and drew near to the house, he heard music and dancing. And he called one of the servants and asked what this meant. And he said to him, 'Your brother has come, and your father has killed the fatted calf, because he has received him safe and sound.' But he was angry and refused to go in. His father came out and entreated him, but he answered his father, 'Lo, these many years I have served you, and I never disobeyed your command;

yet you never gave me a kid, that I might make merry with my friends. But when this son of yours came, who has devoured your living with harlots, you killed for him the fatted calf!' And he said to him, 'Son, you are always with me, and all that is mine is yours. It was fitting to make merry and be glad, for this your brother was dead, and is alive; he was lost, and is found.'"

What Happens Next?

CAST

Player-1

Player-2

Player-3

Player-4

Player-5

Storyteller-1

Storyteller-3

Crowd-1

Crowd-2

Crowd-3

Crowd-4

Crowd-5

Storyteller-2

Narrator

[Just prior to the beginning of this dramatization, there has been a dramatic enactment of the parable of the Prodigal Child from the fifteenth chapter of Luke's Gospel by Player-1, Player-2, Player-3 and a Narrator. The Narrator reads the Gospel while Player-1, Player-2, and Player-3 act out the story as a narrative mime.]

SCENE ONE

CROWD-1:

Well, if you ask me, that isn't a very good story!

STORYTELLER-2:

What do you mean it isn't a very good story?

CROWD-1:

> I mean that is no way to end a story!

STORYTELLER-1:

> What's wrong with it?

CROWD-1:

> We're left up in the air. The younger son is blowing it all off at the party, oblivious to the conflict around him. The older son is "mad as hell and isn't going to take it anymore." The parent is on the back porch unsuccessfully trying to reconcile the two kids.

STORYTELLER-3:

> So?

CROWD-1:

> So, we're left hanging. What happens next?

STORYTELLER-2:

> What do you think happens next?

SCENE TWO

CROWD-1:

> Well, I can imagine what a typical American family would have done.

STORYTELLER-1:

> What typical American family?

CROWD-1:

> The Cleavers on "Leave It to Beaver."
> [Crowd-1 brings Crowd-2 up to the platform and presses Story-teller-2 and Storyteller-3 into service for "Scene Two." They take the same positions that Player-1, Player-2 and Player-3 finished up in.] O.K., now, I'll be Wally. [To Crowd-2] You be the Beav. [To Sto-ryteller-2 and Storyteller-3] And you two be June and Ward. O.K., here goes.

STORYTELLER-3:

> Hi, honey, I'm home.

STORYTELLER-2:

Oh, hi, dear. How was your day?

STORYTELLER-3:

Peachy keen, June. How was your day?

STORYTELLER-2:

It was really going super until trouble hit.

STORYTELLER-3:

Uh-oh! What kind of trouble, dear?

STORYTELLER-2:

The boys aren't talking to each other. I think you'd better speak to them.

STORYTELLER-3:

O.K. fellows, what seems to be the problem?

CROWD-2:

Wally's pickin' on me, Dad! Just because you didn't send me to bed for a month without dinner after I ran away from home and then came back, Wally won't talk to me or play with me anymore! I think he wishes that I got eaten by cannibals or something.

STORYTELLER-3:

Wally, is that true?

CROWD-1:

Well....

STORYTELLER-3:

Well what?

CROWD-1:

Well, Beaver gets away with murder and nothing ever happens to him.

STORYTELLER-3:

Beaver didn't commit murder, Wally, just grand larceny. Now are you going to hold that against him for the rest of his life or this television series...whichever comes first?

STORYTELLER-2:

Come on, boys. Let's show the entire American viewing audience how the Cleavers can forgive and forget.

STORYTELLER-3:

What do you say, fellas?

CROWD-1:

Oh, all right. I forgive you, Beaver.

CROWD-2:

And I'm sorry, Wally, for all the horrible things I've done to you off camera and the nerdy friends I've taken into your room to destroy it. I promise to be the best younger brother a fella could ever have. [They hug.]

STORYTELLER-2:

Don't they make you proud, Ward?

STORYTELLER-3:

That's our boys, June! [They all freeze.]

SCENE THREE

CROWD-3:

Wait a minute! Wait a minute! Is there a physician in attendance? I think I'm going to have a saccharine attack.

STORYTELLER-2:

What's your problem?

CROWD-3:

What we just saw. That's twenty years old. It's too unrealistic. Forgiveness needs more than a weekly thirty-minute episode if it is really going to occur. I just don't believe that's what happened next.

STORYTELLER-3:

Oh yeah? Well what do you think happened next?

CROWD-**3**:

I think "Dallas" or "Dynasty" could give us an idea of what happened next.

STORYTELLER-**2**:

What on earth do you mean? Show us!

CROWD-**3**:

All right, I will. What happens next is colored by revenge and surprising unexpected twists. Now I'll need some help. [Crowd-3 brings Crowd-4 and Crowd-5 up from the congregation and puts them in the final positions of Player-1, Player-2 and Player-3. Storyteller-2, Storyteller-3, Crowd-1 and Crowd-2 sit down.] I'll be the plotting younger child. [To Crowd-4.] You'll be the older child who seems to forgive but never forgets. [To Crowd-5.]You be the dottering old idiot of a parent. Now here's what's been happening. Mom is still in seventh heaven because I'm back. Sis is keeping her own counsel but seems to have adjusted to my annoying presence back home. But I'm not content. I'm trying to get Sis to plot with me so we can have all that the Old Lady has left.

CROWD-**4**:

So, you really pulled the wool over her eyes, didn't you?

CROWD-**3**:

Listen, Sis, she's got more than one loose screw rolling around up there. She bought my story hook, line and sinker. If you ask me, her elevator doesn't go all the way to the top. The lights are on but nobody's home.

CROWD-**4**:

So?

CROWD-**3**:

So, she's dangerous. She's a nuisance. She's an easy touch for the first smooth-talking operator who comes along. And then what will be left of the family fortune?

CROWD-**4**:

I suppose you have a point there. But what do you want me to do?

15

CROWD-3:

Just co-sign this piece of paper with me.

CROWD-4:

What will that do?

CROWD-3:

It will secure a permanent place for Mumsie-pooh in the Swiss Home for seriously deranged cuckoos! Just put your John Hancock right on the dotted line. Two family members testifying to the fact she's lost her marbles is enough to get rid of her for life.

CROWD-4:

And then?

CROWD-3:

And then it's all ours, Sis! Come on, are you going to let lightning strike twice in the same place?

CROWD-4:

Oh, all right! [Crowd-4 signs the piece of paper.]

CROWD-3:

Great! Now relax and let me break the bad news to her. [Crowd-3 whistles and Player-4 and Player-5 come in dressed, in white caps and white coats. Crowd-5 comes alive and moves toward Crowd-3.]

CROWD-5:

What is it, son?

CROWD-3:

I see a permanent vacation in your immediate future. Take a good look at this! [Crowd-3 shows Crowd-5 the signed piece of paper.]

CROWD-5:

Oh my God! Son, how can you do this?

CROWD-3:

To protect you from yourself, Mummy dearest, and to protect our best interests from you. Guards, take her away!

CROWD-**5**:

[To Crowd-4.] But don't you see? If he'd do this to me, how long before he'd do the same thing to you? For God's sake, both of you, come to your senses!

CROWD-**3**:

All right, guards, I've heard enough. It's "hasta la bye-bye" time. Get her out of here!

CROWD-**5**:

[As Player-4 and Player-5 carry her off.] I love you both. I know you'll both come to your senses. Write when you get a chance!

CROWD-**3**:

[Wiping his hands clean.] Well, Sis, now that she's out of the way, it's all ours! Everything she had is ours!

CROWD-**4**:

What do you mean ours?

CROWD-**3**:

Well, I mean, it was, after all, my idea. So, I thought we could split it all right down the middle. Half for you and half for me.

CROWD-**4**:

But you've already spent your half, little brother! What's left is mine. All mine!

CROWD-**3**:

What a comedian! You really have a sense of humor, Sis!

CROWD-**4**:

You know something else? I think Mom was right.

CROWD-**3**:

About what?

CROWD-**4**:

If you'd do it to her, you would do it to me! Little brother, I've just made another decision.

17

CROWD-5:

What's that?

CROWD-4:

You're a liability around here. You're not a very good risk. So, little brother, I want you off my property by morning!

CROWD-3:

But what will I do?

CROWD-4:

I don't know and I really don't care. Say, maybe you could get your old job back feeding pigs! [The characters freeze.]

SCENE FOUR

PLAYER-2:

Well that's as bizarre, in its own way, as the first one was.

PLAYER-3:

Why don't we let the characters speak for themselves and tell us what happened next? [Player-1, Player-2 and Player-3 assume their original positions and freeze. Crowd-3, Crowd-4 and Crowd-5 sit down with the congregation. The technique which will be used in "Scene Four" is that one character will move freely while speaking. The characters that are being addressed, however, remain frozen like statues.]

[Player-3 goes to Player-2.] I could kill you, you little conniving, double-talking jerk! She bought your story, didn't she? I despise you and all your irresponsible, free-loading friends who think life is a joke and just one big party! It's hard to believe you're my little brother. But I want you to know I've learned something from all of this. Those you love and trust can turn on you and hurt you the most. I'll be more cautious next time. [Player-3 goes back to his original place and freezes.]

PLAYER-2:

[Player-2 goes to Player-3.] You have a right to be upset with me. I understand your anger. If our roles were reversed, I'd be angry at

18

you. But I miss you, brother. I miss your presence. I miss your experience. I miss your kidding. I miss your not so tongue-in-cheek corrections. I miss your love. I hope some day you will forgive me too.

[Player-2 goes to Player-1.] I didn't mean to hurt you when I left. I needed to go. I needed to explore. There's a big world out there! I'm not really sure why I even came back, except that I was hungry and had no place else to go. And you were so happy to see me. Why? How, in God's name, could you possibly let me come back after what I'd done? I think that question will haunt me 'til the day I die. [Player-2 goes back to his original position and freezes.]

PLAYER-1:

[Player-1 goes to Player-2.] Look at him: free spirited, not afraid to take a chance, hopeless dreamer, and quite an actor. I don't forgive you because you're genuinely sorry. I forgive you, I love you, because I can't do anything else. You are my son. [Player-1 goes back to her original position and freezes.]

PLAYER-3:

[Player-3 goes to Player-1.] He always gets everything! Why am I always left out? I've been slaving here, doing everything you asked me to do. I think you've always liked him better. What's so bad about being responsible? Do nice guys always have to finish last? I think I've learned an important lesson. No more Mr. Nice Guy for me! [Player-3 goes back to his original position and freezes.]

PLAYER-1:

[Player-1 goes to Player-3.] Look at him: faithful, dependable, a little too serious at times but always there when I need him. Don't you realize that there's plenty of room in my heart for both of you? You've seen parts of me your younger brother will never know. I've shared with you my weakness, my fears, my hurt, as well as my longings and dreams. I forgive you for your stubbornness and your resentment. I forgive you for your lack of understanding. I love you because I can't do anything else. You are my son. [Player-1 goes back to her original position and freezes.]

SCENE FIVE

[Storyteller-1, Storyteller-2, Storyteller-3, Crowd-1, Crowd-2, Crowd-3, Crowd-4, Crowd-5, Player-4 and Player-5 all come up to the acting area.]

STORYTELLER-2:

Three versions of what might have happened next.

STORYTELLER-3:

But the most important question still remains...

ALL:

What do you think happens next? [Here all characters freeze as an instrumental version of "Amazing Grace" begins to be played. After a verse, all the players slowly and quietly return to the congregation.]

—FINIS—

PROPS

1. One (1) pen to be used in Scene Three.

2. One (1) piece of paper to be used in Scene Three.

3. One (1) whistle for use in Scene Three.

4. Two (2) white hats for Player-4 and Player-5 to wear in Scene Three.

5. Two (2) white coats for Player-4 and Player-5 to wear in Scene Three.

PRODUCTION NOTES

The first time this biblical drama was performed, I had a woman play the part of the Parent and two men play the parts of the Older Child and the Younger Child. The three characters, who mimed the action of the parable (Player-1, Player-2 and Player-3) as the gospel was proclaimed, later assumed the identity of their character in Scene Four. It is important that in each rendition of "What Happens Next?"

the principal characters assume the final gospel positions of the Parent, the Older Child and the Younger Child.

In the cast of characters, Player-4 and Player-5 only appear in Scene Three. You may choose to have these roles played by characters who have parts in other scenes. There is nothing magical about the number of characters in these biblical dramas. I always created enough parts for the number of Biblical Explorers working with me that particular quarter of the academic year at Santa Clara University. You could perform this biblical drama with significantly fewer people, if you so desire.

I oftentimes use the device of having the players or characters come out of the congregation. The Biblical Explorers are generally students and staff at the University with no extraordinary dramatic expertise. Most of our time and energy goes into reflecting, discussing and dramatically playing with the biblical stories. Less time is devoted to the practice and performance of the biblical dramas. By having the players come from the congregation, my hope is that the congregation will come to realize two things. First of all, the Word of God in worship is located in the midst of the people of God. Secondly, the players are people like themselves. There is nothing more effective or powerful than peers preaching to peers. Therefore I encourage you, if you do this biblical drama within a worship context, to have the dramatic players come from the congregation and return to the congregation at the conclusion of the drama.

When this biblical drama was created and first performed, "Dallas" and "Dynasty" were two popular weekly evening soap operas. Since television programs tend to go through an infinite number of reruns, I suspect that the references to these television shows will be understood. If you find that your dramatic group suggests you change the references, by all means do so. This is an excellent way to adapt this biblical drama to your purposes. And when your group makes production choices like that, it is another way they invest themselves in the biblical drama and make the process and production more their own.

REFLECTION QUESTIONS AND EXERCISES

1. I invite you or your reflection group to go back to the beginning of the fifteenth chapter in Luke's Gospel. Read the first three verses. "The tax collectors and the sinners, however, were all crowding round to listen to him, and the Pharisees and scribes complained saying, "This man

welcomes sinners and eats with them.' So he told them this parable."
(New Jerusalem Bible)

What insight into Jesus' character do you get from these biblical verses? What type of person is Jesus? How would you answer that question from the perspective of a scribe or Pharisee? How would you answer that question from the perspective of a sinner or a tax collector?

Remember that "behaviors" incarnate and reflect "attitudes." What do you learn about the character and attitude of Jesus through his behavior in the fifteenth chapter of Luke's Gospel? Explain. What insight do you get into the characters of the sinners, tax collectors, scribes and Pharisees from their respective behaviors in the fifteenth chapter of Luke's Gospel? Explain. What insight do you get into the characters of the Parent, the Older Child and the Younger Child from their behaviors and attitudes in the parable Jesus told from the fifteenth chapter of Luke's Gospel? Explain.

If you were a sinner or a tax collector in the audience, what would be a good ending to this story of "The Prodigal Child" for you? Explain. If you or your reflection group were a scribe or a Pharisee in the audience, what would be a good ending to this story of "The Prodigal Child" for you? Explain. If you or your reflection group were the Parent in the story that Jesus told, what would be a good ending of the story for you? Explain. If you or your reflection group were the Younger Child in the story Jesus told, what would be a good ending of the story for you? Explain. If you or your reflection group were the Older Child in the story Jesus told, what would be a good ending of the story for you? Explain.

2. There are three parables of God's mercy that Jesus tells in the fifteenth chapter of Luke's Gospel. The parable of "The Prodigal Child" is the only one of the three that doesn't really have an ending. We have to decide imaginatively how the story ends. I invite you or your reflection group to creatively explore how this story from the Gospels might end.

In your reflection group, what does each member of your group imagine happened next? What attitudes of the different characters are revealed through their behaviors that are part and parcel of each imagined ending? What do you learn about the Parent through your imagined ending? Explain. What do you learn about the Older Child through your imagined ending? Explain. What do you learn about the Younger Child through your imagined ending? Explain. What do you learn about yourself through your imagined ending? Explain.

Now I invite you or your reflection group to brainstorm and come up with some answers to the following questions. What might be some humorous or comic endings to this story? What makes these endings humorous or comic? Explain. What might be some serious or tragic endings to this story? What makes these endings serious or tragic? Explain. How would Alfred Hitchcock have ended this story? Explain. If this story had been an episode of the Rod Serling television series "The Twilight Zone," how would he have ended the story? Explain. What other types of endings can your group imagine? Explain. Remember: There's no "right" or "wrong" answer to these questions. They are invitations to imaginatively explore and play with biblical texts in order to potentially discover new insight into them.

3. Imagine that you are the Younger Child of the Parent in this story. Insert yourself into this story and discover some of the details that are not given to us. What prompts you to leave home? What do you experience in that "distant land"? What prompts you to "come to your senses"? What are your thoughts, feelings and physical sensations throughout your adventures? What kind of a person is your parent in this story? What kind of a person is your older brother or sister in this story? What kind of a person are you in this story?

4. Try and think of experiences in your life where you have resented someone or something. What caused the resentment? What does resentment do to you personally? How does an attitude of resentment find expression in behavior? Does resentment change the person to whom it is directed? If so, how? If not, why not? Explain. Does resentment change the person who feels it for another person? If so, how? If not, why not? Explain.

Try and think of experiences in your life where you have forgiven someone. What motivated you to forgive him/her? What does forgiving another person do to you personally? Does the act of forgiveness change you? If so, why? If not, why not? Explain.

Try to think of experiences in your life where you have been forgiven by someone. What had you done that required forgiveness? What do you think motivated that other person to forgive you? What did the experience of being forgiven do to you personally? Does the experience of being forgiven change you? Are your attitudes and behaviors any different after you have been forgiven than they were before you were forgiven? If so, why? If not, why not? Explain.

5. There are three characters in this biblical story: a parent, an older child and a younger child. Which of these three characters do you like most? What do you like in that person? Explain. Which of these three characters do you like least? What do you most dislike about that person? Explain. Which of these three characters do you identify with most? Explain. Which of these three characters do you identify with least? Explain.

Imagine that these three biblical characters symbolize or represent parts of you. What part of you does the younger child represent? Explain. What part of you does the older child represent? Explain. What part of you does the parent represent? Explain.

There are three major characters in Scene Four of this biblical dramatization: a parent, an older child and a younger child. Which of the characters in this scene do you like most? What do you like about that character? Explain. Which of the characters in this scene do you like least? What don't you like about this character? Explain. With which character do you identify most? Explain. With which character do you identify least? Explain. If you looked upon these three characters as symbolizing parts of yourself, what part of you would the older child in this biblical drama symbolize? Explain. What part of you would the younger child in this biblical drama symbolize? Explain. What part of you would the parent in this biblical drama symbolize? Explain.

6. Imagine that you and your reflection group are newspaper reporters. Your newspaper is doing a feature article on this incident that Luke describes in the fifteenth chapter of his Gospel. You are sent to interview each of the three major characters involved. Spend some time brainstorming together on the following exercise. What questions would you like to ask each of these characters? Write them all down. How do you imagine that each character might reply in response to these questions? Write those responses down. Does any question or any response surprise you? Why or why not? Explain. Do you learn anything new about any of the characters from the responses that you imagine they would give to your proposed questions? Why or why not? Explain.

This is another way that you can proceed. As a group do some brainstorming on all the questions you would like to ask these three major characters. Then have three members of your group assume the characters of the Parent, the Older Child and the Younger Child. I recommend you have the Parent sit between the two children. Then have some of the other members of your group assume the identity of newspaper reporters. Have the reporters put your questions to them and listen to how the characters respond. If new questions suggest themselves to you as a result of any answers that the characters give, be sure to ask those new questions also. After the interview, reflect together on the following questions. Did any question or any response surprise you? If so, why? If not, why not? Explain. As a result of this interview format, did you get any new insight into the characters of this biblical story? If so, what are those insights? If not, why not? Explain.

7. I invite you or your reflection group to undertake a journal exercise. You will need a journal and a pen or pencil. First of all, read the biblical story of "The Prodigal Child" with the Younger Child in mind. Jot down words you would use to describe the attitudes and behaviors of this character in the story. Secondly, read the biblical story again with the Older Child in mind. Jot down words you would use to describe the attitudes and behaviors of this character in the story. Thirdly, read the biblical story once more with the Parent in mind. Jot down words you would use to describe the attitudes and behaviors of this character in the story. Now take some time and share the words that each member of your group has written down to describe: (a) the Younger Child, (b) the Older Child, and (c) the Parent. Did what you wrote or what you heard others wrote give you any insight into these characters? Why or why not? Explain. Do you ever exhibit any of the attitudes or behaviors of the characters in this biblical story? Explain.

8. In Scene Four of the biblical dramatization, what is the Older Child's description and evaluation of the Younger Child? Do you agree or disagree with this description and evaluation? Explain. What is the Older Child's description and evaluation of the Parent? Do you agree or disagree with this description and evaluation? Explain.

In Scene Four of the biblical dramatization, what is the Younger Child's description and evaluation of the Older Child? Do you agree or disagree with this description and evaluation? Explain. What is the Younger Child's description and evaluation of the Parent? Do you agree or disagree with this description and evaluation? Explain.

In Scene Four of the biblical dramatization, what is the Parent's description and evaluation of the Younger Child? Do you agree or disagree with this description and evaluation? Explain. What is the Parent's description and evaluation of the Older Child? Do you agree or disagree with this description and evaluation? Explain.

Now that you have read and reflected on both the biblical story and the biblical dramatization, I invite you to write three cinquains: one on the Older Child, one on the Younger Child, and one on the Parent. A cinquain is a five-line piece of poetry. The first line consists of the word that is the subject or title of the poetic reflection. The second line consists of two descriptive adjectives that deal with your subject. The third line consists of three participles (i.e. action words, verbs ending in "ing") that capture active dimensions of your first line subject. The fourth line consists of a four-word descriptive phrase that summarizes your subject. The fifth line consists of a one-word restatement of your first line subject. The final line/word usually brings out some nuanced dimension of the first line/word and is an emphatic or gentle restatement of it.

After you have written a cinquain on the Younger Child, the Older Child and the Parent, share these cinquains with the other members of your reflection group. Since the three stories or parables found in the fifteenth chapter of Luke's Gospel are often referred to as parables of God's mercy, I encourage you and your reflection group to write one final cinquain on "mercy." When you have finished, share what you have written with the other members of your reflection group. What did you discover about mercy from your own cinquain or those composed by the other members of your reflection group? Explain.

2. Peter's Confession About Jesus

(Matthew 16:13-20)

Now when Jesus came into the district of Caesarea Philippi, he asked his disciples, "Who do men say that the Son of man is?" And they said, "Some say John the Baptist, others say Elijah, and others Jeremiah or one of the prophets." He said to them, "But who do you say that I am?" Simon Peter replied, "You are the Christ, the Son of the living God." And Jesus answered him, "Blessed are you, Simon Barjona! For flesh and blood has not revealed this to

you, but my Father who is in heaven. And I tell you, you are Peter, and on this rock I will build my church, and the powers of death shall not prevail against it. I will give you the keys of the kingdom of heaven, and whatever you bind on earth shall be bound in heaven, and whatever you loose on earth shall be loosed in heaven." Then he strictly charged the disciples to tell no one that he was the Christ.

Who Do You Say They Are?

CAST

Player-1 (Brian)	Narrator
Player-2 (Jim)	Crowd-1
Player-3 (Pam)	Crowd-2
Player-4 (Ed)	Crowd-3
Player-5 (Denean)	Crowd-4
Player-6 (Judy)	Crowd-5
Player-7 (Craig)	Crowd-6
Inner-6	Inner-7

SCENE ONE

NARRATOR:

Good evening, ladies and gentlemen, and welcome to another edition of "Who Do You Say They Are?" From the beginning of time people have revealed who they are by what they say and what they do. This is the program where we show you, the studio audience, contemporary vignettes of human experience and have you decide what a character has revealed of himself or herself. So, without further ado, let's get on with some contemporary revelations.

Our first scene involves Brian.

29

[Player-1 comes out and sits down on a chair. Player-1 looks very sad.]

He's recently gotten some very bad news. Jim is about to discover this bad news. Let's see what he reveals of himself through this discovery.

[Narrator goes back upstage while Player-2 comes on and moves in Player-1's direction.]

PLAYER-2:

Say, Brian, what's happening?

PLAYER-1:

Oh, not much.

PLAYER-2:

Are you going to the big "we've made it through the quarter" party over at Marty's tonight?

PLAYER-1:

No, I don't think so.

PLAYER-2:

Why not?

PLAYER-1:

Oh, I don't know. I just don't feel much like partying.

PLAYER-2:

What's wrong with you, man? Why do you look so glum?

PLAYER-1:

I just got some bad news.

PLAYER-2:

You're flunking calculus.

PLAYER-1:

No, worse than that.

PLAYER-2:

You're flunking calculus, art appreciation and religious studies.

PLAYER-1:

No. I think I could even handle that.

PLAYER-2:

What's wrong then?

PLAYER-1:

I just found out my mom's got cancer. The doctor says she's got less than six weeks to live.

PLAYER-2:

[Obviously affected, sighs. He sits down next to Player-1 and gradually puts his arm around Player-1's shoulder.]

Oh no, man, I'm sorry. I'm really sorry.

NARRATOR:

Let's freeze it right there.

[Player-1 and Player-2 hold their positions.]

Now, you in the studio audience be the judges. What does Jim reveal of himself in this situation? What do you say, ma'am?

CROWD-1:

I think he shows compassion. I'm surprised a peer could be that compassionate.

NARRATOR:

And you, sir, what do you say?

CROWD-2:

He's obviously gay.

NARRATOR:

I beg your pardon?

CROWD-2:

You know. He's a homosexual, a flaming fag!

31

SCENE TWO

NARRATOR:

Let's move on to our second scenario.

[Player-1 and Player-2 leave the platform area and sit down. Player-3 and Player-4 move onto the platform area and sit down on two chairs or stools.]

Pam and Ed are preparing for some pretty tough midterm exams. Let's see what we learn about Denean as she encounters this pre-occupied pair.

PLAYER-3:

Why is it that we always seem to be preparing for a midterm?

PLAYER-4:

I think one of my psychology professors explained that it will help us face our midlife crisis some day.

PLAYER-3:

I'm an accounting major and I still can't understand the logic or arithmetic of four midterms in one quarter.

PLAYER-4:

It's new math, Pam.

[Player-5 comes in.]

PLAYER-3:

Hi, Denean.

PLAYER-4:

What's up? You may take that as an essay or multiple choice question.

PLAYER-5:

Studying for midterms?

PLAYER-4:

Elementary, my dear Watson. As the good book says: "Midterms, like the poor, you will always have with you."

PLAYER-3:

Where are you off to?

PLAYER-5:

There's a woman from Nicaragua who's speaking about the plight of the oppressed in her country.

PLAYER-4:

She must have been a Business or Engineering major.

PLAYER-5:

No. She's going to speak about what the Sandinista government has been doing for the poor people of her country.

PLAYER-3:

I don't know, Denean. I've still got studying to do and I don't understand the whole situation down there very well.

PLAYER-5:

Neither do I, and I'm afraid of what I don't know. I'd like to try to understand. That's why I'm going.

PLAYER-4:

What's there to understand? You've got a bunch of Mattel Communist Guerillas, the Darth Vaders of the Universe, that the Russians wind up and have take over a country.

PLAYER-5:

I don't think it's that simple or that clear, Ed. If you were poor, and your children needed food, clothing, and shelter, and a government offered you all of this, do you really think you'd mind whether that government espoused capitalism or communism?

NARRATOR:

Hold it right there!

[The players freeze.]

OK, audience, now it's your turn. What does Denean reveal of herself here? What do you say, ma'am?

CROWD-3:

I think she's a communist sympathizer who could better use her time preparing for midterms.

NARRATOR:

And you, sir?

CROWD-4:

I think she's someone who's concerned and interested about events and circumstances that affect people in other parts of the world.

NARRATOR:

Two very different perceptions of what Denean revealed. Let's move on to a third scenario.

SCENE THREE

[Player-3, Player-4 and Player-5 move off of the platform as Player-6 and Inner-6 move onto the platform. Player-6 sits down. Inner-6 will represent and speak what Player-6 is really thinking. Inner-7 will represent and speak what Player-7 is really thinking. It will be important to dramatically convey this through positioning of the "other selves."]

Please observe Craig. Notice the self he reveals to Judy and the self only he knows. He is about to meet Judy.

INNER-6:

Oh-oh, he's looking at you! He's probably a statistics major and has figured out the total number of skin blemishes on your face.

INNER-7:

There's that girl again. I wish I knew her name. I think I'll just walk over there and have dinner with her. She'd probably choke or have heart arrest. Well, at least you could wave.

[Player-7 waves.]

You don't have to look so interested.

[Player-7 catches himself.]

That's it. Act as if any of these lovely coeds would die to have you dine with them.

[Player-7 starts walking toward Player-6.]

PLAYER-7:

Do you mind if I sit down?

PLAYER-6:

No, not at all.

INNER-6:

I only think it fair, however, to warn you that I have leprosy.

PLAYER-7:

Hi. I'm Craig.

INNER-6:

I can tell she's not impressed with your name. You'd better score some points fast if you don't want her to throw up her dinner right in your face.

PLAYER-7:

What's your name?

INNER-6:

Lie! Then you can tell him later that the girl he met was your ugly stepsister who accidentally kissed a frog at an early age and has been bewitched ever since.

PLAYER-6:

My name is Judy. Where are you from, Craig?

INNER-7:

Actually, Judy, I'm a Klingon on a "search and destroy" mission.

PLAYER-7:

I'm from....

INNER-7:

If you say Martinez she'll laugh at you.

35

PLAYER-7:

... the Bay area. Where are you from?

PLAYER-6:

I'm from ...

INNER-6:

Lie!

PLAYER-6:

... the Bay area too. Are you going to the dance tonight?

INNER-7:

He wouldn't miss it. He's the comic relief. He's clumsy when he doesn't drink. He's so uncoordinated on the dance floor that he holds the distinction of being Arthur Murray's most stunning failure.

PLAYER-7:

Yeah, I'll be there. Will you?

INNER-6:

Lie! I'm warning you.

PLAYER-6:

Yeah, so will I. I've got to go now.

[Player-6 gets up to leave.]

Maybe I'll see you there.

INNER-6:

You'd better set your phasor for stun.

[Player-6 holds out her hand to Player-7. Player-7 hesitates shaking it.]

INNER-7:

Oh, you're really cool, Craig. Shake her hand, you idiot! What do you think she has? Leprosy?

PLAYER-7:

Ah, nice talking with you, Judy. See you tonight.

NARRATOR:

The action freezes right there.

[Player-6, Player-7, Inner-6 and Inner-7 freeze in their places.]

And now we move to our audience for their judgment. You, sir, what do you think Craig revealed of himself here?

CROWD-5:

He's a Cromagnon Nerd! He's a genetic mistake. If he were a computer program, I would erase him!

NARRATOR:

And you, ma'am?

CROWD-6:

I think he's a shy young person desperately afraid of rejection by someone he's attracted to.

SCENE FOUR

NARRATOR:

Thank you very much. It's time now, viewers, to move back in time and catch a glimpse of how a person from the past revealed who he was by what he said and did. Tonight's subject: Jesus Christ. He was considered a monster by some and Messiah by others.

[Player-1, Player-2, Player-4, Player-6 and Inner-7 move to one side of the platform. Player-3, Player-5, Player-7, Inner-6 and Crowd-5 move to the other side of the platform.]

Let's hear what people of his day had to say about who he was.

PLAYER-4:

I was a tax collector. He called me down from a tree. He gave me back my self-respect. He spent an evening eating, drinking and storytelling with me and my friends. None of us were ever the same.

PLAYER-7:

He was a glutton and a drunkard!

PLAYER-6:

For thirteen years I was stooped over, crippled, a prisoner of my own body. Then one day he touched me. He healed me. He released my shackled spirit.

PLAYER-3:

And he did it on the Sabbath. He was a lawbreaker!

PLAYER-2:

I was not an educated person but he made me—he made all of us—feel important. His words were good news to all of us poor.

INNER-6:

He was an agitator, a disturber. He wanted to undermine the social order as we knew it. He was a dangerous revolutionary!

PLAYER-1:

I was dead and he brought me back to life.

PLAYER-5:

Only God is Lord of life. He had a Messianic complex!

INNER-7:

I denied him three times and he forgave me.

CROWD-5:

He was a blasphemer! Only God can forgive sins!

[Here all the players freeze. The Narrator comes down to the center of the acting area.]

NARRATOR:

So there were and continue to be differences of opinion. Please tune in next week for another edition of the show that asks that haunting question: "Who do you say they are?" Until next time, this is your host, Garth Ashbeck, saying: "Who do *you* say you are?"

—FINIS—

PROPS

1 Four (4) chairs or four (4) bar stools to be used and arranged on the platform for the different scenes.

2. One (1) small bench (preferably without a back) for use in Scene One.

PRODUCTION NOTES

A remarkable little document entitled *Fulfilled in Your Hearing: The Homily in the Sunday Assembly* was produced by the National Conference of Catholic Bishops. It proposes that one of the principal goals of those who preach is to make "connections." The homilist draws on his prayerful study of scripture, his reflection on human experience and his communication skills to help people see the "connection" between the reality of the biblical story and the reality of their own life.

This biblical dramatization embodies the attempt of the Biblical Explorers to do just that for their worship community. In examining the questions of Jesus in this biblical story, we considered the ways by which we ourselves reveal who we are. We drew upon some dramatic dictums. First of all, characters reveal who they are by what they say and what they do. Secondly, characters can equivocate with their words. It is very difficult for characters to sustain physical lies.

What is true of dramatic characters is also true of biblical characters and ourselves. We reveal who we are through our words and actions. Therefore, we tried to discover who Jesus revealed himself to be by examining both his actions and his words in the Gospel. Hopefully through the biblical dramatization "Who Do You Say They Are?" we invited the congregation to do the same.

The behaviors of human beings can be interpreted positively or negatively by those who observe them. We often reveal more of ourselves through these evaluations than we do about the significance or meaning of the actions by which we are judged. If this is true in our life, it is equally true in the life of Christ.

The names of the characters used in this dramatization are the names of the Biblical Explorers who helped create this drama and played a particular role. A simple form of adaptation would be to change these scripted names to those of the people who are working with you on the production of this biblical dramatization.

Most of the human experiences that find expression in these biblical dramatizations are drawn from the lives of the students, faculty and staff who live and work there. They are of universal significance. The compassion of God surprises us and touches us in life in many ways. As we deal with the unexpected death of loved ones, the fears experienced in beginning new relationships, the struggle to move out of provincial concerns to life in a global community, that compassion comes to us through human hands and eyes and hearts. Because of the shapes and forms it comes in, God's presence and compassion all too easily escape our notice without the assistance of regular reflection on these human experiences. Hopefully these biblical dramatizations can assist you in calling your reflection groups and worshiping congregations to such an awareness.

REFLECTION QUESTIONS AND EXERCISES

1. In the biblical story (Matthew 16:13-20), Jesus' first question to his disciples is: "Who do people say that I am?" The responses of the disciples are three: (a) John the Baptist, (b) Elijah or Jeremiah, or (c) one of the prophets. I invite you and your group to reflect and share on the following questions.

Who was John the Baptist? What did John the Baptist say? What did John the Baptist do? What did John the Baptist symbolize or represent to the people of his day? What do you think he symbolized or represented to the early Christian community?

What attitudes and behaviors of John the Baptist do you think people found in Jesus? What accounts for some people thinking Jesus was John the Baptist?

Who were Elijah and Jeremiah? What did Elijah say? What did Elijah do? What did Jeremiah say? What did Jeremiah do? What did Elijah symbolize or represent to the people of his day? What did Jeremiah symbolize or represent to the people of his day? What do you think Elijah symbolized or represented for the early Christian community? What does he symbolize or represent for you and your group? What do you think Jeremiah symbolized or represented for the early Christian community? What does he symbolize or represent for you and your group? What attitudes and behaviors of Elijah or Jeremiah did people find in Jesus? Explain.

What do you and your group think are some of the attitudes and behaviors of prophets? What do prophets say? What do prophets do? Why would people of Jesus' own time think he was a prophet? What was there about Jesus' words and actions that was prophetic? Do you and your group think there was a prophetic dimension to Jesus' words and actions? Explain. Are those who follow Jesus supposed to be prophetic in their words and actions? Why or why not? Explain. If there is a prophetic dimension to being a Christian, how can we incarnate this prophetic dimension of word and action in our society today? Explain.

2. I invite you and your reflection group to become detectives. Your goal is to try to build up a profile of Jesus' character by piecing together the clues you discover by reading one of the synoptic Gospels (i.e. Matthew, Mark or Luke). Remember the principle that characters reveal who they are by what they say and what they do. As you move through the Gospel story, what does Jesus reveal of himself through his words and his actions? Which of his words strike each member of your reflection group? What is it about them that strikes you? What tone of voice do you imagine Jesus using when he says these words? Explain. Which of his actions strike each member of your reflection group? What is it about them that strikes you? Explain.

When you have carefully listened to all the clues that people found in the Gospel, what overall character sketch of Jesus do you get from this Gospel? You can extend this exercise in a different way by contrasting and comparing the picture of Jesus we get in Mark's Gospel with the pictures we get from Matthew's and Luke's Gospels. In what ways are the pictures similar? In what ways are their portraits of Jesus, based upon his words and actions, different? If there are differences, what accounts for these differences? Explain.

3. Images of Christ emerge throughout the history of Christianity that somehow respond to the challenges and needs of each culture, each society and each age. I invite you and your group to consider the following pictures or images of Jesus and share what they mean to you.

In what ways is Christ a Lawgiver?
In what ways is Christ the Mercy of God?
In what ways is Christ the Judgment of God?
In what ways is Christ a Redeemer?
In what ways is Christ the Word-Made-Flesh?

41

In what ways is Christ Emmanuel (God-with-us)?
In what ways is Christ the Son of God?
In what ways is Christ a Teacher?
In what ways is Christ a Healer?
In what ways is Christ a Servant?
In what ways is Christ a Forgiver of Sins?
In what ways is Christ the Compassion of God?
In what ways is Christ a Prophet?
In what ways is Christ a Risen One?
In what ways is Christ a Liberator?
In what ways is Christ a Parable of God?

What other images of Christ would you add to this? Which images or pictures of Christ mean most to you? Explain. Which images or pictures of Christ mean least to you? Explain. Which images or pictures of Christ do you find most comforting? Which images or pictures of Christ do you find most challenging?

4. The second question that Jesus addresses to his disciples is: "Who do you say that I am?" There is a dramatic shift in focus. Previously they had reported who other people thought he was. Now they were each asked to consider who *they* thought he was. We only have a record of Simon Peter's reply (Mt 16:16).

Ernesto Cardenal has given us a great treasure in his four-volume work entitled *The Gospel In Solentiname* (New York: Orbis Press, 1984). He records there the reflections of his small community to the various scriptural passages. Oscar, a member of the faith community, answers Jesus' second question in the following way: "For me, he is the one who is making me change, since I came to know him... And he has united me with others. And he is the one who keeps us united in this community. He has brought us together" (Vol. II, p. 223).

I invite you and your reflection group to each consider this second question that Jesus put to his disciples. There is no right or wrong answer. Each person's response will be unique to his/her experience. So, spend some time considering this question: Who do you say that Christ is for you? When you have allowed sufficient time for people to reflect on this question, invite the members of your group to take turns sharing their responses to this question. They can begin their sharing in any way. You might suggest the following simple formula: "For me, Christ is...."

5. St. Teresa of Avila wrote a beautiful prayer about the way Christ is present after his resurrection. It was put to music by John Michael Talbot on his album *Heart of the Shepherd*. The words of the prayer are:

Christ has no body now but yours,
no hands, no feet on earth but yours.
Yours are the eyes through which he looks
with compassion on this world.
Yours are the feet with which
he walks to do good.
Yours are the hands with which
he blesses all the world.
Yours are the hands.
Yours are the feet.
Yours are the eyes.
You are his body.
Christ has no body now but yours,
no hands, no feet on earth but yours.
Yours are the eyes through which he looks
with compassion on this world.
Christ has no body now on earth but yours.

I invite you and your reflection group to go through St. Teresa's prayer and discuss the implications of each thing she affirms. What do you and your reflection group think of Teresa's basic assertion that "Christ has no body now on earth but yours"? What does she mean by this? Do you agree or disagree with her evaluation? Explain. What does it mean to be Christ's hands? What are some of the ways in which we can be Christ's hands? Explain. What might be some of the ways that Christ blesses the world through our hands? Explain. What does it mean to be Christ's feet? What are some of the ways in which we can be Christ's feet as he walks to do good? Explain. What does it mean to be Christ's eyes? What are some of the ways Christ uses our eyes to look with compassion on this world? Explain.

6. Gerard Manley Hopkins was a Jesuit poet. In one of his pieces of poetry entitled "As Kingfishers Catch Fire" his final lines explore the mystery of Christ's presence in the world. Hopkins writes:

Christ plays in ten thousand places,
Lovely in limbs, and lovely in eyes not his
To the Father through the features of men's faces.
[*Hopkins* edited by Graham Storey. London: Oxford University
Press, 1967, p. 85.]

What do you and your reflection group think Gerard Manley Hopkins
meant by these lines? Think of some of the people in your life who have
embodied Christ's presence and love for you. Who are these people?
What was there about them that made them an *alter Christus,* "another
Christ," for you? What were their Christlike qualities? Explain.

7. How are the first three scenes in the biblical dramatization related to
the last scene? Explain. What happens in Scene One of the biblical
dramatization? Have you ever had to deal with death in your life? Has
anyone close to you ever had to deal with death in his/her life? What
were your thoughts, feelings and physical sensations? What did you
learn about your attitude toward death through your actions? What did
you learn about your friends' attitudes toward death through their
actions? What do you think about Player-2's reaction to Player-1's sad
news? If you had been Player-1's roommate or friend, how would you
have reacted? What do you think about Crowd-1's evaluation of Player-
2's reaction? Explain. What do you think about Crowd-2's evaluation
of Player-2's reaction? Explain.

What type of character does Player-3 reveal herself to be through her
attitude and behavior in Scene Two? Explain. Who does Player-4 reveal
himself to be through his attitude and behavior in Scene Two? Explain.
Who does Player-5 reveal herself to be through her attitude and behavior in Scene Two? Explain. What do you think about Crowd-3's evaluation of Player-5? Explain. What do you think about Crowd-4's
evaluation of Player-5? Explain.

Have you ever experienced "inner voices" like those found in Scene
Three? Why or why not? Explain. Can some of those "inner voices" be
positive as well as negative? Why or why not? Explain. Which voices is
it easier to pay attention to? Explain. Who does Player-6 reveal herself
to be through her attitude and behavior in Scene Three? Explain. Who
does Player-7 reveal himself to be through his attitude and behavior in
Scene Three? Explain. What do you think about Crowd-5's evaluation

44

of Player-7? Explain. What do you think about Crowd-6's evaluation of Player-7? Explain.

8. The biblical title "Son of God" most likely implies a sonship which is adoptive. Because we are chosen by God a special relationship is established between God and us *(New Jerome Biblical Commentary)*. St. Paul spoke of the attitudes and behaviors of those who are chosen by God and therefore in this special relationship with God. I invite you and your reflection group to consider the meaning of the attitudes and behaviors St. Paul articulates in his letter to the Colossians (Col 3:12-17).

What does it mean to be "chosen" by God? What does it mean to be a son or daughter of God? What are the ways we reveal this relationship through our words and actions? How can God's loving us change us or affect us? What does it mean for us to be clothed in sincere compassion? What does it mean for us to be clothed in kindness? What does it mean for us to be clothed in humility, gentleness and patience? Why does St. Paul talk about these attitudes or virtues in terms of clothing or things we wear?

Do you find it easy or difficult to forgive others when a quarrel begins? Explain. What makes it easy or what makes it difficult? Explain. What does St. Paul mean by saying that the Lord has forgiven us? What has the Lord forgiven us? Why is the Lord's forgiveness a reason for forgiving others?

Why do you think "love" keeps all the other attitudes and virtues together and completes them? How does "love" do this? What do you think "the peace of Christ" is? What happens when the peace of Christ reigns in our heart? What happens when it doesn't?

Why is thankfulness so important to St. Paul that he mentions it at least twice in this small passage of his letter? What are the behaviors or actions that reveal the attitude or virtue of thankfulness? When in your life have you been thankful? When in your life have you been thankless? What do you think the relationship is between "remembering" and "thanksgiving"? Did you know that the Greek word for "thanksgiving" is *eucharistia?*

What do you and your reflection group think is "the message of Christ"? What would it mean for "the message of Christ, in all its richness, to find a home in you"? Explain. What does it mean to teach one another? What do we teach one another? How do we teach one another? What does it mean to advise one another in all wisdom? Can you remember anyone ever giving you some wise advice? What was it? How and why was this advice full of wisdom? Explain. Can you remember anyone ever giving

45

you some foolish advice? What was it? How and why was this advice foolish? Explain. How do you know the difference? Are there any guidelines? What would some of those guidelines be?

Why is it important to give shape and expression to our gratitude? In what ways do you express your gratitude or thanks? Have you ever experienced saying things or doing things in the name of the Lord? Why or why not? Explain. Why not attempt for twenty-four hours to consider what Christ might say and consider what Christ might do as you meet people and go through the experience of a day. Reflect on what was hard or difficult about this. Does saying or doing things in the name of the Lord sometimes or oftentimes change what we say and do? Why or why not? Explain.

3. Signs of Things To Come

(Luke 21:5-19)

And as some spoke of the temple, how it was adorned with noble stones and offerings, he said, "As for these things which you see, the days will come when there shall not be left here one stone upon another that will not be thrown down." And they asked him, "Teacher, when will this be, and what will be the sign when this is about to take place?" And he said, "Take heed that you are not led astray; for many will come in my name, saying, 'I am he!' and

'The time is at hand!' Do not go after them. And when you hear of wars and tumults, do not be terrified; for this must first take place, but the end will not be at once." Then he said to them, "Nation will rise against nation, and kingdom against kingdom; there will be great earthquakes, and in various places famines and pestilences; and there will be terrors and great signs from heaven. But before all this they will lay their hands on you and persecute you, delivering you up to the synagogues and prisons, and you will be brought before kings and governors for my name's sake. This will be a time for you to bear testimony. Settle it therefore in your minds, not to meditate beforehand how to answer; for I will give you a mouth and wisdom, which none of your adversaries will be able to withstand or contradict. You will be delivered up even by parents and brothers and kinsmen and friends, and some of you they will put to death; you will be hated by all for my name's sake. But not a hair of your head will perish. By your endurance you will gain your lives."

To Rule the Earth with Justice

CAST

Chorus
Self (Cari)
Voice-1
Voice-2
Voice-3
Voice-4
Person-1 (Marcy)
Person-2 (Bren)
Person-3

Student-1
Student-2
Student-3
Student-4
Student-5 (Ed)
Student-6 (Shannon)
Student-7 (Ellen)
Person-4

SCENE ONE

[The five characters that are part of this scene, Self, Voice-1, Voice-2, Voice-3 and Voice-4, take their places on the platform. Then the Chorus comes out and lights one of the large standing candles.]

CHORUS:

The Lord will come to rule the earth with justice. [Chorus then goes and sits back down and the action of Scene One begins.]

SELF:

[The phone rings. Self answers it and begin to talk with her

49

mother. Four other players will represent the voices of pressures she feels in her life.]

Hi, Mom. What a surprise. I didn't expect to hear from you.... What do you mean, "What do I mean?" I meant it's a nice surprise.... What am I doing? Oh, getting ready for finals and the end of the quarter.... How's school? Well...[Here Voice-1 begins to speak to Cari and distract her in her conversation.]

VOICE-1:

Yeah, Cari, tell Mom how you're doing. You dropped one class. You're going to take "incompletes" in two other classes. And is anybody offering odds on whether you pass "Statistics"? From Freshman Honors to Academic probation in one quarter. Quite a slide! Disneyland ought to have a ride named after you!

[Voice-1 continues to speak to Cari but she mimes the conversation.]

SELF:

Money? Funny you should ask.

[Here Voice-2 begins to speak to Self and distracts her.]

VOICE-2:

Ask your mother if she knows how to spell "overdrawn." Tell her how some of your financial aid has been withdrawn. Tell her about your father deciding not to give you the money he promised you because he thinks it will develop "strength of character" in you. Ask her how it feels being the mother of a third world debt.

[Voice-2 continues to speak to Self but she mimes the conversation.]

SELF:

Am I making some nice friends at school?

[Here Voice-3 begins speaking to Self and distracts her.]

VOICE-3:

Go ahead, Cari, tell Mom about your roommate moving out because of "irreconcilable differences." Tell her how your boyfriend dropped you because he found someone who didn't look like the Queen of the Soybean Festival. Tell her how you couldn't bribe someone to take you to the boat dance. Tell her how the people on your floor treat you like the winner of the "Leper of the Month" contest. Tell her...

[Voice-3 continues speaking to Self but mimes the conversation.]

SELF:

How's life in general?

[Here Voice-4 begins speaking to Self and distracts her.]

VOICE-4:

Go ahead, Cari, tell her "it sucks." You can't eat. You can't sleep. You don't know how to study. You fall asleep in class. You couldn't find the Mission Church even if you wanted to go to Mass. You have no social life. The counseling department says the earthquake didn't cause your stress, it just exaggerated it. Face it, Cari, they think you're a cuckoo!

[Here Voice-4 continues speaking to Self but mimes the conversation.]

SELF:

Well, it's been great talking to you, Mom, but I've got to go. Love you too.

[Self hangs up and the Voices continue talking to her. Instead of words they use the sounds "Wah wah" and gradually build in intensity. Self finally yells at them.]

Shut up!

[Self gathers them up and puts them behind the curtain. Self breathes deeply and then opens the curtains to hear them speaking their "Wah wahs" again. Self pulls one of the pressures inside and closes the curtain.]

Now sit down, and shut up! I will deal with you one at a time!

[Here the players freeze and the Chorus comes out and lights another standing candle. After lighting the candle Chorus speaks.]

51

CHORUS:

The Lord will come to rule the earth with justice.

[After this, all of the players in Scene One sit down and the players for Scene Two take their places.]

SCENE TWO

STUDENT-1:

I can't believe this happened to me.

STUDENT-2:

I can't believe this happened to me.

STUDENT-1:

I thought I was prepared.

STUDENT-2:

I thought I was prepared.

STUDENT-1:

Maybe I should drop this class.

STUDENT-2:

Maybe I should drop this class.

STUDENT-1:

I could see a tutor.

STUDENT-2:

I could see a tutor.

STUDENT-1:

What should I do?

STUDENT-2:

What should I do?

[Student-1 and Student-2 freeze.]

STUDENT-3:

I can't believe this happened to me.

STUDENT-4:

I can't believe this happened to me.

STUDENT-3:

He told me not to worry.

STUDENT-4:

She told me not to worry.

STUDENT-3:

We didn't need protection.

STUDENT-4:

We didn't need protection.

STUDENT-3:

I'm not sure I want a baby.

STUDENT-4:

I'm not sure I want a baby.

STUDENT-3:

Maybe I should get some advice.

STUDENT-4:

Maybe I should get some advice.

STUDENT-3:

Maybe I should face this alone.

STUDENT-4:

Maybe I should face this alone.

STUDENT-3:

What should I do?

STUDENT-4:

What should I do?

[Student-3 and Student-4 freeze.]

STUDENT-5:

[Student-5 and Student-6 are on the stage talking together when Student- 7 comes by.]

Hi, Ellen. Where are you off to in such a hurry?

STUDENT-7:

I'm going over to Benson to sign up for the Oxfam fast.

STUDENT-5:

What's the Oxfam fast?

STUDENT-6:

Organized anorexia, if you ask me.

STUDENT-7:

It's a one-day fast run by Oxfam International to help people become more aware of hunger in the world.

STUDENT-5:

How do they do this?

STUDENT-6:

By having people starve themselves.

STUDENT-7:

Actually, Ed, students are invited to fast for twenty-four hours. In this way we choose to experience hunger for a brief period of time. For most of the world's hungry it is not a "choice," it's a way of life. Would you like to do it, Shannon?

STUDENT-6:

Sounds like a devious way for Marriott to get out of fixing us meals. What good would it do?

STUDENT-7:

Besides the important awareness and understanding it creates, Marriott donates the money of the meals given up during the fast to Oxfam International. This money collected all over University campuses goes to alleviate hunger in our world. Would you like to come with me and sign up, Ed?

STUDENT-5:

I'm not really sure.

STUDENT-6:

Listen, Ed, the fast is on a Thursday. Your classes are on Thursday and go an hour and forty-five minutes. How could you sit there for that long with your stomach growling?

STUDENT-5:

Part of me would like to, Ellen, but I just don't know. What should I do?

[Student-5, Student-6 and Student-7 freeze and then all of the players of Scene Two come out of their freeze and speak to different parts of the audience.]

ALL:

You make the call!

[All players freeze again as the Chorus goes and lights another large standing candle.]

CHORUS:

The Lord will come to rule the earth with justice.

[All of the players from Scene Two go back to their places in the congregation and the players from Scene Three come on to the acting area of the platform.]

SCENE THREE

PERSON-1:

[Person-1 is carrying a paper.]

Bren, what are you doing here?

PERSON-2:

[Person-2 is also carrying a newspaper.]

I'll bet the same thing as you, Marcy.

PERSON-1:

I haven't ridden a bus since I was a kid.

PERSON-2:

It's going to be a different experience without my car.

PERSON-1:

How are you doing?

PERSON-2:

I'm from Montana and this just doesn't happen in Montana. Fires, yes. Floods, yes. Blizzards, yes. Twisters, occasionally. Earthquakes, never! I was reading in the paper that the Marina really was hard hit. Your family lives there. How are they doing?

PERSON-1:

I just came from there. They lost some china and some other family antiques, but their home is fine and they'll be O.K. I'd be O.K. if I could figure out how to get home from here on the bus.

[At this point Person-3 comes up and joins them at the bus stop.]

PERSON-3:

Excuse me, is this the Metro bus stop?

PERSON-2:

You've got it, pal. Where are you going?

PERSON-3:

I live here in the Marina and we've pretty much figured out what property and possessions were lost or damaged. I'm trying to get my Insurance Adjustor right now. Would either of you know how to get downtown from here?

PERSON-1:

In a car, "yes." On the bus, I'm afraid not.

PERSON-2:

Looks like we're all in the same boat.

[At this point Person-4 comes up to the bus stop and Person-1, Person-2 and Person-3 begin to engage Person-4 in conversation.]

PERSON-3:

How'd you do in the quake?

PERSON-4:

Not bad at all.

PERSON-1:

Much damage?

PERSON-4:

I didn't lose anything.

PERSON-2:

That's unbelievable.

PERSON-1:

God, are you lucky!

PERSON-4:

I guess so.

PERSON-3:

You don't have to make any insurance claims?

PERSON-4:

No.

PERSON-3:

I'd love to be in your shoes.

PERSON-4:

Yeah. Well…what are you all doing here at the bus stop?

PERSON-1:

Bren and I are trying to get home in the Sunset district.

PERSON-3:

I'm trying to get downtown to see my Insurance Agent.

PERSON-2:

None of us know which bus to take. Would you?

PERSON-4:

Yeah, I think so. To get downtown just catch No. 40. Ask the driver to tell you when to get off to pick up No. 17 downtown. He'll give you a transfer. And you two just catch one of the No. 6 Expresses. That will take you right down Sunset Boulevard. Actually, here come the buses you need now.

[Person-1, Person-2 and Person-3 mime getting on the buses and leaving.]

PERSON-1:

Thanks a lot.

PERSON-2:

Yeah, thanks for the help.

PERSON-3:

Aren't you coming?

PERSON-4:

No, I think I'll just sit here and read the papers for a while. Are you finished with them?

PERSON-2:

Yeah, they're all yours.

[Person-1, Person-2 and Person-3 start to take off and freeze.]

PERSON-4:

Thanks. Hmmm. Earthquake Aid pours in from around the country. Outpouring of Community Care to the victims of the earthquake. That's great!

[Person-4 turns the page.]

Federal spending for the homeless cut 5%.

[Person-4 just shakes his head and then lies down on the bus stop bench putting the papers over him as a blanket. When he is settled down, the Chorus comes out and lights the last remaining unlit large standing candle.]

CHORUS:

The Lord will rule the earth with justice.

[Lights fade and players from Scene Three go back to their places in the congregation. Allow some moments of quiet reflection. It could also be appropriate to have some live or recorded music as background for these moments of reflection.]

—FINIS—

PROPS

1. Four (4) large standing candles to be placed at different points in the congregation near the acting area so that when they are lit they will be visible to all in the congregation.

2. Matches or one (1) taper with which to light the large standing candles at the different moments in the biblical dramatization.

3. One (1) phone which will be used in Scene One.

4. One (1) bench that can be used in Scene Two and is needed for Scene Three.

5. Two (2) or three (3) bar stools which can be used in Scene One and Scene Two.

6. Two (2) newspapers which are used by characters in Scene Three.

PRODUCTION NOTES

This biblical dramatization was created and first performed at the end of a fall term at Santa Clara University. The scripture passage from the Gospel of Luke is that for the thirty-third Sunday in Ordinary Time. This worship celebration falls at the end of Ordinary Time and just before the Christian community enters into the season of Advent.

Since the readings for this Sunday dealt with "signs," the Biblical Explorers tried to make a connection between the significance and meaning of signs in the biblical reading and the significance and meaning of signs in their life experience. The challenge in both cases is to develop the ability to see the signs and understand them.

The quarter system in a university setting is a very accelerated form of education. I have found, as a teacher and a counselor, that it often produces unnecessary and unhealthy stress in students. The end of quarters with the approaching "day of judgment," to use a biblical image to describe the educational experience of final examinations, is an even more pressurized and stressful time for these same students. This will give you the context of the first scene from the biblical dramatization.

In the second scene we attempted to balance the personal crisis with a more global issue. All three of the brief vignettes in this second scene deal with signs and the challenges of understanding them and responding to them in an appropriate manner.

In the third scene the Biblical Explorers attempted to incorporate the experience in the Bay Area of the Loma Prietta earthquake. An interesting twist was the addition or insertion of the continuing disaster called "homelessness" within a consideration of the effects of the natural disaster called an "earthquake." Hopefully you will be confronted by both the challenge (i.e. hunger, homelessness) and the promise (i.e. "The Lord will come to rule the earth with justice") that are part of this biblical passage, biblical dramatization and liturgical season.

You will notice the stage direction that players come onto a platform. That direction is there because all of these biblical dramatizations were first performed in the Mission Church of Santa Clara University at the 10:00 PM Sunday student liturgy. The Mission Church has a small six to eight inch raised platform upon which the ambo and altar are placed. Since everything and everyone are on the ground level, this makes it somewhat easier to have a focus. I usually have this platform cleared except for the lectern, and the players use this space of slight elevation for the enactment of the biblical dramatization. You will also notice the stage direction that players come from the congregation and return to the congregation. This embodies my belief that the Word of God is situated in the midst of the people of God. That Word, that proclamation, comes from the community and returns to the community. It is fitting that the ministers of that Word event do the same.

REFLECTION QUESTIONS AND EXERCISES

1. This scripture passage from Luke (21:5-19) talks about signs. How good are you and your reflection group at reading signs? What are some of the signs that you have seen most recently? What do those signs mean? What happens to people who disregard traffic signs? When people don't pay attention to traffic signs, is that healthy or unhealthy, safe or dangerous? Explain. What is the goal of traffic signs? Explain.

What are the signs or indications of the current natural season of the year? What do these signs say to you? How do you understand and interpret them? What are some examples of the ways you respond to these signs? Explain.

What are signs that you are hungry? What are some healthy ways to pay attention to these signs? What happens if you don't pay attention to these signs or respond to them for a long period of time? Is that dangerous? Is that harmful? If so, why? If not, why not? Explain. What do people do who experience these signs of hunger but simply don't have the means (e.g. money) to appropriately satisfy that hunger? What do they do? Do you and your reflection group think that individuals or groups of people who have more than enough means to respond to their own needs have a moral or ethical responsibility to assist those with insufficient means to respond to their needs? If so, why? If not, why not? Explain. In relation to this consideration, you and your reflection group might consider 2 Corinthians 8:1-24. I especially encourage you to focus on verses 8-15. Does St. Paul shed any light on what might be an appropriate Christian response to the needs of others? If so, what forms or shapes might that response take in our day and age? Explain.

What are the signs that you are tired? What are some healthy ways to pay attention to these signs? When you experience some of these signs what would be an example of an appropriate response? What happens if you don't pay attention to these signs or respond to them for a long period of time? Is that dangerous? Is that harmful? If so, why? If not, why not? Explain.

2. What are some of the signs of good physical health? Name as many of them as you and your reflection group can. Why are these signs of good physical health? Explain. What are some of the signs of

poor physical health? Name as many of them as you and your reflection group can. Why are these signs of poor physical health? Explain. Is physical exercise good for the health of the body? If so, why? If not, why not? Explain. Name as many of your favorite forms of physical exercise as you and your reflection group can.

In what sense can stress be a sign? What would be some of the ways to understand and interpret this sign? What do you and your reflection group think might be some appropriate ways of responding to this sign? Explain. Have you ever known anyone who experienced stress? What do you think was the cause or causes that produced this stress? Explain. If you could have advised this person on how to rid himself/herself of this stress, what practical suggestions would you have made? Explain. Have you ever personally experienced stress? What do you think was the cause or causes that produced this stress? Explain. Did you pay attention to the stress? If so, why? If not, why not? Explain. What good advice could you give yourself now to rid yourself of stress or avoid stress in the future? Explain.

In what sense can a heart attack be a sign? What would be some healthy and appropriate ways to respond to this sign? Explain. What will happen if a person doesn't pay attention to this sign? Explain.

What are some signs of good spiritual health? Name as many signs as you and your reflection group can. Why are these signs of good spiritual health? Explain. What are some signs of poor spiritual health? Name as many signs as you and your reflection group can. Why are these signs of poor spiritual health? Explain. Can spiritual exercise be good for one's spiritual health? If so, why? If not, why not? Explain. Name as many forms of spiritual exercises as you and your reflection group can.

It could be both educational and spiritually profitable for different members of your reflection group to take turns (over a period of weeks or months) teaching and leading the rest of the reflection group in one of their favorite forms of spiritual exercise.

3. This particular Gospel passage (Lk 21:5-19) is part of the liturgy for the thirty-third Sunday in Ordinary Time during Year C of the liturgical cycle. I invite you and your reflection group to explore the meaning of the liturgical year as a means of coming to appreciate the particular

character and contribution of Ordinary Time to the experience of the liturgical calendar.

What do you and your reflection group think Advent is all about? How many weeks does Advent last? Since it is a season of preparation, what does Advent prepare us for?

What do you and your reflection group think Christmas is all about? How many weeks does Christmas last? Since Jesus came into this world almost two thousand years ago, what do you think we really celebrate at Christmas?

What do you and your reflection group think Lent is all about? How many weeks does Lent last? Since it is a season of preparation, what does Lent prepare us for?

What do you and your reflection group think Easter is all about? How many weeks does Easter last?

What do you and your reflection group think Pentecost is all about? How many weeks does Pentecost last?

What do you and your reflection group think Ordinary Time is all about? How many weeks does Ordinary Time last? What kind of time is the Christian community predominantly called to celebrate? What do you think the Church may be saying to us or inviting us to respond to by having us celebrate Ordinary Time for over half of the liturgical year?

While I invite you and your reflection group to consider the following questions about Ordinary Time, you could also explore them profitably with the other liturgical seasons of the year. Remember that often there is no "right" or "wrong" answer. You are simply invited to imaginatively explore these questions as a means of delving deeper into the possible meaning of the liturgical season.

What are the colors of Ordinary Time?
What are the sounds of Ordinary Time?
What are the smells of Ordinary Time?
What are the tastes of Ordinary Time?
What are the touches of Ordinary Time?

What does Ordinary Time tell us about where God is to be experienced or found in our life, our relationships and our world?

If you were to draw Ordinary Time what would you put in that picture? Draw it.

If you were to sing Ordinary Time what would that song sound like? What type of song would it be? Sing it.

If you were to dance Ordinary Time what kind of dance would it be? Dance it.

If you were to tell the story of Ordinary Time what kind of story would it be? Tell the story.

4. In this biblical passage from the Gospel of Luke, the same Jesus who has met controversy throughout his ministry and especially in Jerusalem now predicts the same treatment for his disciples (New Jerome Biblical Commentary). St. Paul wrote to the Corinthian community about the trials of an apostle. I invite you and your reflection group to consider what St. Paul's words might mean for Christians today. Slowly and meditatively read over 2 Corinthians 6:3-13. Allow some quiet time of reflection. Slowly and meditatively read over this passage again. Once more allow some quiet time of reflection. Slowly and meditatively read over this passage for a third time. Again allow some quiet time of reflection. Now reflect and share together on the following questions.

As apostles and disciples, how might we give people an occasion to stumble or criticize our mission? As followers of Christ constantly shaped by the spirituality of the gospels, what do you and your reflection group think our mission is? Could there be times that we are criticized when we may be doing the right thing? How should we regard criticism in these cases? Is this the criticism that St. Paul was speaking about?

What do trials, hardship, affliction, floggings, imprisonment, riots, fatigue, sleepless nights and days of hunger mean in our culture and society? Do you think people reading or hearing these words in the first world and the third world hear different things? Do those of us in the first world tend to understand St. Paul's descriptions in a more figurative way? If so, why? If not, why not? Explain.

Do people in developing countries tend to experience and understand St. Paul's description in a more literal way? If so, why? If not, why not? Explain. I strongly encourage you to explore the book *El Sal-*

vador: A Spring Whose Waters Never Run Dry (1990 by Ecumenical Program on Central America and the Caribbean [EPICA], 1470 Irving St. N.W., Washington, D.C. 20010. U.S.A.). It is a collection of testimonies from the Christian base communities which have been gathered over the past ten years. From refugee camps, shanty towns and communities in war zones, Salvadoran Christians speak about their lives and their work in building a more just society. I think their stories and their words will crack open new meaning and understanding of St. Paul's description of the trials of the apostolate from a developing nation's perspective.

How do we prove that we are true ministers of God by our endurance in the face of these trials? Explain. What are the weapons of justice? How do apostles fight with the weapons of justice? What might it mean for apostles to attack with the weapons of justice? What might it mean for an apostle to defend with the weapons of justice?

What are some of the times and ways that apostles can be honored? What are some of the times and ways that apostles can be insulted? Was Jesus honored in his life and ministry? When? How? Why? Was Jesus insulted in his life and ministry? When? How? Why? If we are the followers of Jesus, do you think we should be suspicious if we never experience insult in the living and exercising of our Christian ministry? If so, why? If not, why not? Explain.

What do you think St. Paul means by saying "we are regarded as liars although we speak the truth"? What might this mean for us in our Christian life and ministry? What do you think St. Paul means by saying "we are regarded as unknown though we are well known"? What might this mean for us in our Christian life and ministry?

What do you think St. Paul means by saying "we are regarded as dead and yet we live"? What might this mean for us in our Christian life and ministry? Have you ever experienced the paradox St. Paul spoke of when he wrote "we appear to be afflicted, but we remain happy"? What is the nature of those afflictions? Where does that happiness come from? Have you ever experienced the paradox St. Paul spoke of when he wrote "we seem to be poor, but we enrich many"? If so, how? If not, why not? Explain.

5. Who does the character Self reveal herself to be in Scene One through what she says and what she does? Remember that in the theater behaviors reveal attitudes. What are Self's behaviors in this scene? What attitudes does she reveal through her behaviors? Does her behavior change as the scene progresses? If so, why? If not, why not? Explain. Do her attitudes change as the scene progresses? If so, why? If not, why not? Explain.

What are the pressures that are affecting Self in Scene One? I invite you and your reflection group to name each one of them. If you were in Self's place, how would these Voices or pressures affect you? How does Self respond to these Voices or pressures? What does Self reveal of her character by the way she responds to the Voices? Explain.

The Voices in Scene One may or may not correspond to some of the pressures in your own life. What are the Voices that evaluate you and always catch you up short in your life? What are the pressures that you are attempting to respond to in your life right now? In naming and sharing some of these with the other members of your reflection group, you may find that others are also dealing with the same pressures or Voices. What is "one step" that you can take to begin dealing with these pressures or Voices in your life?

6. In Scene Two, where is Student-6 going? Have you ever heard of the Oxfam fast? What is it? What is the goal of the Oxfam fast? [You can get educational information from *Oxfam America,* 26 West St., Boston, MA 02111. You can also call them toll free at 1-800-OXFAMUS.] Have you ever done anything to become more aware of hunger in the world? If so, what? If not, why not? Explain.

Who does Student-5 reveal himself to be through his actions? What attitudes do his behaviors reveal? Who does Student-7 reveal herself to be through her actions? What attitudes do her behaviors reveal? Who does Student-6 reveal herself to be through her actions? What attitudes do her behaviors reveal? Scene Two ends with Student-5 trying to decide what to do. What do you and your reflection group think that Student-5 should do? You make the call. Explain why you think he should do this. What would you do if you were in his position? Explain.

In Scene Three, where is Resident-1 going? Where is Resident-2 going? Where is Resident-3 going? Where is Resident-4 going? Who does Resident-4 reveal himself to be through his words and actions? Who has the knowledge that is needed in order for Resident-1, Resident-2 and Resident-3 to get home or downtown? Who has the knowledge or wherewithal to get Resident-4 home? Explain.

7. What do you and your reflection group think is the significance of the Chorus lighting a candle four times during the biblical dramatization? Do you and your reflection group see any connection between the words of the Chorus (i.e "The Lord will come to rule the earth with justice" [Ps. 97:9]) and the action of the Chorus (i.e. lighting one of the large standing candles)? Explain.

Pope John Paul II once said, "If you want peace, work for justice." What do you think he meant by this statement? What is the relationship between "peace" and "justice"? How can a person in our culture and society be a peacemaker? Explain. How can a person in our culture and society work for justice? How many ways does this biblical dramatization suggest that one could work for justice? Explain.

St. Ignatius of Loyola in his *Spiritual Exercises* offers the exercitant three powerful reflection questions for periodic consideration in prayer. Those three questions appear in the first spiritual exercise (no. 53). They appear at the end of a spiritual exercise as a suggested conversation from the heart with Christ on the cross looking down at the one praying. Those three reflection questions are: (1) What have I done for Christ? (2) What am I doing for Christ? (3) What ought I to do for Christ?

I would like to adapt these three questions based on the themes of this biblical dramatization. I encourage you to use them for personal reflection and for the shared faith process of your group. To give you a context for understanding these questions, I invite you to consider in your reflection group whether justice found a place in Jesus' life and ministry. Did Jesus work for justice? If so, why? If not, why not? Explain. How did Jesus work for justice in his life and ministry? If justice was an important dimension of Jesus' life and ministry, should it find a proportionately important place in the life and ministry of those who follow in his footsteps? If so, why? If not, why not? Explain. The adapted reflection questions that I propose are: (1) How have I worked for justice? Where have I worked for justice in my life, my relationships, my community and my world? (2) How am I working for justice? Where am I working for justice in my life, my relationships, my community and my world? (3) How ought I to work for justice? Where will I work for justice in my life, my relationships, my community and my world?

8. I invite you and your reflection group to create a cinquain (i.e. a five-line piece of poetry) on "signs" and another cinquain on "ordinary time." Remember that the first line consists of the word that is the title of the poetic reflection (i.e. either "signs" or "ordinary time"). The second line consists of two descriptive adjectives that deal with your subject. The third line consists of three participles (i.e. action words, verbs ending in "ing") that capture active dimensions of your first line subject. The fourth line consists of a four word descriptive phrase that summarizes your subject. The fifth line consists in a one-word restatement of your first-line subject. The final line/word usually brings out some nuanced dimension of the first line/word and is an emphatic or gentle restatement of it. After you have written your cinquains on "signs" and "ordinary time" share them with the other members of your reflection group. What new insights do you get into "signs" or "ordinary time" from what you have written? Explain. What new insights do you get into "signs" or "ordinary time" from what the other members of your reflection group have written? Explain.

4. The Ten Bridesmaids

(Matthew 25:1-13)

"Then the kingdom of heaven shall be compared to ten maidens who took their lamps and went to meet the bridegroom. Five of them were foolish, and five were wise. For when the foolish took their lamps, they took no oil with them; but the wise took flasks of oil with their lamps. As the bridegroom was delayed, they all slumbered and slept. But at midnight there was a cry, 'Behold, the bridegroom! Come out to meet him.' Then all those maidens rose and trimmed their lamps. And the foolish said to the wise, 'Give us some of your oil, for our lamps are going out.' But the wise replied, 'Perhaps there will not be enough for us and for you; go rather to the dealers and buy for yourselves.' And while they went to buy, the bridegroom came, and those who were ready went in with him to the marriage feast, and the door was shut. Afterward the other maidens came also, saying, 'Lord, Lord, open to us.' But he replied, 'Truly, I say to you, I do not know you.' Watch therefore, for you know neither the day nor the hour.'"

Hey, Wake Up!

CAST

Voice

Narrator

Crowd-1

Crowd-2

Noah

Captain

Passenger

President

Reporter

Jesus

Goat

Peasant

Host

Guest-1

Guest-2

Roomie-1 (Ann)

Roomie-2 (Matthew)

Student-1 (Brennan)

Student-2 (Laura)

Student-3

Student-4 (Christi)

Parent (Mr. Swanberg)

Speaker

SCENE ONE

[All of the Players for Scene One go to their positions on the platform and freeze. There are four brief vignettes in the scene which will come to life one at a time and then go back into a frozen position until the scene has ended. When all the Players are in position, a Voice is heard.]

VOICE:

"Five of them were foolish, while five of them were wise."

71

NARRATOR:

Welcome to "Great Moments in the Foolishness of the World."

[Movietone background music would be very appropriate.]

It doesn't take a genius to realize that the twentieth century has no corner on foolishness. Who will ever forget that flood of foolishness demonstrated by some Middle East neighbors centuries ago.

CROWD-1:

Hey, Noah, trying to corner the market on lumber? What in the world are you doing?

NOAH:

I'm building an ark.

CROWD-2:

Well, this is the biggest recreation vehicle I've ever seen. I didn't know you studied mechanical engineering. Do you have a permit for this?

NOAH:

No, not exactly.

CROWD-1:

Hey, what's that smell? What are you doing with all these animals?

[Crowd-1 points to the congregation.]

CROWD-2:

Looks like you're partial to even numbers. Maybe he collected them in pairs because he's going into the breeding business.

CROWD-1:

Don't you think collecting stamps or coins might create less of a stink and mess in the neighborhood? What's all of this for?

NOAH:

I have it on good authority that we're in for a lot of rain. Maybe even a flood. I don't want to be caught unprepared.

CROWD-2:

Well, you win the "Chicken Little" award, Noah. Good old Mister "Doom and Gloom."

CROWD-1:

Why, there's not a cloud in the sky. What do you mean it's going to rain.

[Thunder is heard. They all look up. Noah takes out an umbrella and opens it. Crowd-1 and Crowd-2 look at each other with puzzlement and confusion on their faces. All of these Players freeze as the Movietone theme is heard.]

NARRATOR:

Speaking of boats, let's jump ahead a few thousand years. We're on the deck of one of the sleekest sailing vessels ever conceived by human imagination.

PASSENGER:

So, Captain, you must be very proud of your ship.

CAPTAIN:

Indeed I am. It is the finest ship ever built to sail the seas.

PASSENGER:

And how many lifeboats does it carry?

CAPTAIN:

Only a very few. They're really only for decoration.

PASSENGER:

But Captain, what if there was an accident?

CAPTAIN:

Let me assure you, Ma'am, the Titanic is indestructible. It's simply invincible.

[They freeze. The Movietone theme is heard.]

NARRATOR:

Ignorance is also sometimes invincible. Listen in on this presidential press conference.

REPORTER:

President Reagan, what do you plan to do about the homeless in America?

PRESIDENT:

Homeless? There are no homeless in America.

REPORTER:

With all due respect, sir, you only have to look on the streets of every major city and you will see that there are hundreds of thousands of homeless.

PRESIDENT:

Well, I've spoken with my advisors and they have assured me that there are no homeless people in this greatest country of the world.

REPORTER:

Mr. President, do you believe everything you're told?

[They freeze as the Movietone theme is heard.]

NARRATOR:

We conclude our historical look with a peek into the future. "When the Son of Man comes in his glory…all the nations will be assembled before him and he will separate people one from another as the shepherd separates sheep from goats.…Then he will say to those on his left:

JESUS:

"Go away from me with your curse upon you…for I was hungry and you never gave me food; I was thirsty and you never gave me drink; I was a stranger and you never made me welcome, naked and you never clothed me, sick and in prison and you never visited me."

GOAT:

"Wait just a minute! Whoa! Hold on here! Excuse us for not being psychic or clairvoyant! Just give us one example of when we failed to feed you or welcome you or clothe you or visit you!"

JESUS:

"Whenever you failed to do it to the least of your brothers or sisters, you failed to do it to me."

[They all freeze. The Movietone theme is heard again. Then the Players from Scene Two all stand and speak together.]

ALL:

Hey! Wake Up!!!

[The Players from Scene One all return to their places in the congregation and the Players from Scene Two take their positions on the platform.]

SCENE TWO

VOICE:

"The foolish ... brought no oil."

STUDENT-1:

[Wakes up and looks horrible.]

Oh my God, turn your stereo off, Ann, it's making me sick.

ROOMIE-1:

My stereo isn't on.

STUDENT-1:

Then why do I hear the 1812 Overture playing and have cannons going off in my head?

ROOMIE-1:

Maybe that's got something to do with last night.

STUDENT-1:

All I know is that I've got a mondo headache. So please speak very softly.

ROOMIE-1:

Do you remember anything at all from last night?

STUDENT-1:

Like what?

ROOMIE-1:

Like where you were? What you did? How you got home?

STUDENT-1:

> I can feel a sermon coming on. So maybe I had a little bit too much to drink. For crying out loud, since when is it a crime to blow off a little steam?

ROOMIE-1:

> You've been blowing off steam like this every weekend since the beginning of the year. I think you have a problem, Brennan.

STUDENT-1:

> Oh chill out, Ann. Lighten up. Here, have a Bud Light. That ought to mellow you out.

> [Student-1 opens a Bud Light and downs it. Student-1 and Roomie-1 freeze. Roomie-1 then moves to Student-2 who comes to life.]

ROOMIE-1:

> Laura, I'm worried about Brennan.

STUDENT-2:

> What's the matter?

ROOMIE-1:

> I think she has a problem with alcohol.

STUDENT-2:

> You mean because she had too much to drink last night?

ROOMIE-1:

> And the night before that, and the weekend before that for four straight weekends before that.

STUDENT-2:

> It's probably just MSS.

> [Roomie-1 looks puzzled.]

> Midterm Stress Syndrome.

ROOMIE-1:

> But she has these blackouts, Laura. She's can't remember anything about those evenings.

[Student-1 comes in and Roomie-1 and Student-2 look a bit nervous. Student-2 takes out a pack of cigarettes and takes one.]

STUDENT-2:

Anyone got a light?

STUDENT-1:

[Student-1 takes out a Bud Light.]

How about a Bud Light?

[Student-1 downs the beer and all the Players freeze. Then Roomie-1 moves to the Parent who comes to life.]

ROOMIE-1:

I don't really know where to begin, Mr. Swanberg.

PARENT:

Well first off, tell me how "the apple of my eye" is doing. You're Brennan's best friend, Ann. If anyone would know, you would. How's my "little girl"?

ROOMIE-1:

Well, sir, that's what I came to talk to you about.

PARENT:

What's the matter?

ROOMIE-1:

It's Brennan. I think she has a problem and I was hoping you might be able to shed some light on it for me.

PARENT:

You know I'll do anything I can. Hey, speaking of lights, how about a Bud Light?

[Parent offers Roomie-1 a beer and she refuses. He opens one and takes a big drink.]

So what's the big problem, Ann?

ROOMIE-1:

I think Brennan is alcoholic, Mr. Swanberg, and I'm worried

77

about what's going to happen to her if she doesn't get some help real soon.

PARENT:

Oh, Ann, I'm sure she's just blowing off a little steam. I know you're concerned, dear, but there's nothing to worry about. She'll be fine. Just you wait and see.

[Parent and Roomie-1 freeze. Roomie-1, Student-1 and Student-2 join Student-3. There are four chairs to represent the seats of a car. They are positioned two seats in front of the other two seats to create the impression of front seats and back seats of a car. The front seats of the car are facing the center of the congregation.]

ROOMIE-1:

[Student-1, Student-2, Student-3 and Roomie-1 all get into the car.]

I really don't think you ought to be driving, Brennan.

STUDENT-1:

Oh relax, Ann. I'm fine. I've only had a couple of short snorts.

STUDENT-3:

Besides, Ann, it is Brennan's car.

STUDENT-2:

For crying out loud, we're only going to Denny's. It's not even two miles away. What could happen in two miles?

STUDENT-1:

All right, everybody in.

[They all get in and start riding.]

ROOMIE-1:

I still think this is a very bad idea.

STUDENT-1:

That will be noted in the Captain's log. Pilot to Navigator, do you have any humanoid life-form sightings?

STUDENT-2:

No, Captain, the sensors indicate no living life-forms ahead.

ROOMIE-1:

Hey, isn't that a red light straight ahead?

STUDENT-1:

[As Student-1 opens up a Bud Light.]

No! It's a Bud Light.

[Student-1 takes a big drink. There is a sound effect of a car crashing. The occupants are thrown together in slow motion. They slump motionless. Then the sound of a siren is heard. All the Players in Scene Two freeze as the Players from Scene Three stand and speak together.]

ALL:

Hey! Wake Up!!!

[The Players from Scene Two return to their places in the congregation. The Players from Scene Three take their positions on the platform.]

SCENE THREE

VOICE:

"And the door was barred."

HOST:

Welcome everyone to the game show where we gauge the wisdom or foolishness of Santa Clara students' knowledge and perception. And now, contestants, it's time to play: "You Make the Call." Are you ready?

GUEST-1:

Ready.

GUEST-2:

Ready.

HOST:

The category is "Famous Graduates." Ramon Meliam Rodriguez, a graduate of the Santa Clara Business School, went on to become what? You make the call.

GUEST-1:

President of Payne Weber Investment Brokerage?

GUEST-2:

Treasurer of the United States?

HOST:

If you had said: "He went on to become a high level accountant and money lender for Columbian Drug Czar Pablo Escobar," you would have made the right call.

As a follow-up question: Where is he right now? You make the call.

GUEST-1:

On Wall Street?

GUEST-2:

On an extended vacation?

HOST:

Very close. If you had said: "He's in prison," you would have made the right call. Our next category is "Great Greek Gatherings." What activity recently consumed the time and talent of a Greek Chapter on campus? You make the call.

GUEST-1:

Gamma Ray with their naked limbo contest to support World Class Racers of America.

GUEST-2:

Alpha Beta who terrorized neighbors over Halloween to get them to contribute to the Mohandas Gandhi Center for Non-Violence.

HOST:

If you had said: "Sigma Pi who sponsored a Volleyball Tournament at the Dunne Courts to raise money for Aids Research," you would have made the right call. Our next category is "Life After Santa Clara." What have twenty-five members of the class of 1988 done since graduating in June? You make the call.

GUEST-1:

I believe they went to the Hut and are still there.

GUEST-2:

> They all assumed high level positions in Silicon Valley Businesses that are listed in Fortune 500.

HOST:

> If you had said: "They are committing a year of their life in service to the Jesuit Volunteer Corps or Jesuit International Volunteers," you would have made the right call. And now for our final category: "Little Known People from the Bay Area." Former Bay area resident and engineer, Benjamin Linder, helped the villagers of El Cua in Nicaragua develop hydroelectricity. How were his efforts rewarded. You make the call.

GUEST-1:

> Did he get a Nobel Peace Prize?

GUEST-2:

> Was he named an Ambassador of Good Will for the United States?

HOST:

> If you had said: "He was shot in the head point-blank by a group of Contra Rebels," you would have made the right call. One last chance here, contestants. How did the villagers react to his death? You make the call.

GUEST-1:

> Utter foolishness!

GUEST-2:

> A tragic waste!

HOST:

> If you had said: "He inspired the villagers" or had pointed out that the villagers erected a tombstone on his grave with the words "He lit a light that will never be extinguished" engraved on it, you would have made the right call.

> [All the Players from Scene Three freeze. The Players from Scene Four all stand and speak together.]

ALL:

> Hey! Wake Up!!!

[The Players from Scene Three return to their places in the congregation. The Players from Scene Four take their positions on the platform.]

SCENE FOUR

VOICE:

"I do not know you."

ROOMIE-2:

Christi, how was the meeting?

STUDENT-4:

Heavy. It was an informational meeting about hunger in the world, and a lot of what I heard frightened me.

ROOMIE-2:

Like what?

STUDENT-4:

Like everyday 40,00 children die unnecessarily of hunger or hunger-related diseases. Like developing countries are spending more on arms and less on food. Like five multi-national corporations control 90% of all grain that is shipped across national boundaries.

ROOMIE-2:

I'm sorry, Christi, but if you keep this up I'm going to blow a fuse. Besides, I was going to invite you out for some ice cream but I'm quickly losing my appetite.

STUDENT-4:

Thanks, Matthew, but I don't really feel like eating something right now.

ROOMIE-2:

Well, all right. We're still on next Thursday for our pre-Thanksgiving Day dinner, aren't we?

STUDENT-4:

I'm thinking about signing up for the Oxfam fast.

ROOMIE-2:

> What?

STUDENT-4:

> It's taking place on campuses all across the nation the Thursday before Thanksgiving.

ROOMIE-2:

> But why?

STUDENT-4:

> It gives us an opportunity to focus on global inequities and the needs of a hungry world.

ROOMIE-2:

> But all of that is so far away, so unreal. Do you really think fasting will help?

STUDENT-4:

> I know it's just a small gesture, but the philosopher Lao-Tzu said: "A journey of three thousand miles is begun with one step." At least it is a beginning. All they ask is that we give up our meals from Wednesday evening, November 16th, until dinner time on Thursday the 17th.

ROOMIE-2:

> Do you really think we can do something by skipping a few meals in Benson?

STUDENT-4:

> Yes, I do. I want to know more about hunger. I'm afraid that what we don't know can kill people.

ROOMIE-2:

> Well I think the whole idea is a cosmic bummer.

STUDENT-4:

> It's hunger that's the cosmic bummer, Matthew. I was hoping you might sign up with me for the fast.

ROOMIE-2:

> Now Christi, let's be practical. I've got to get ready for finals. I'm

going to need all the energy I can get to keep the old brain cells working. I don't function well on an empty stomach. You really wouldn't want to be around me when I haven't eaten.

[Roomie-2 and Student-4 freeze.]

PEASANT:

[Peasant turns holding a small blanketed baby in his arms. While he speaks in Spanish, an interpreter repeats his lines in English.]

Me llamo Ignacio Osorio.

SPEAKER:

My name is Ignacio Osorio.

PEASANT:

Vengo del pueblo de San Jose en Mexico.

SPEAKER:

I come from the village of San Jose in Mexico.

PEASANT:

Se muere mi nina.

SPEAKER:

My little child is dying.

PEASANT:

No tengo nada para darle a comer.

SPEAKER:

I have no food to feed her.

PEASANT:

Porque usted no me conoce.

SPEAKER:

Because you do not know me.

PEASANT:

Y por eso no lo conozco a usted.

SPEAKER:

> I do not know you.

> [Peasant and Speaker freeze.]

ALL:

> [All the dramatists stand and look at different groups in the congregation as they shout.]

> Hey! Wake Up!!!

—FINIS—

PROPS

1. One (1) Umbrella which will be used by Noah in Scene One.
2. One (1) Captain's Hat which will be used by the Captain in Scene One.
3. One (1) Note Pad and One (1) Pencil or Pen which will be used by the Reporter in Scene One.
4. One (1) Podium or Lectern or Speaker's Stand which will be used by the President in Scene One.
5. Five (5) or Six (6) Cans of simulated Beer which will be used in Scene Two. Cans of Ginger Ale can work very well for this.
6. Four (4) Chairs which will be used in Scene Two for the front and back seats of a car.
7. One (1) Sound Effect of a car crashing.
8. One (1) Sound Effect of a siren.
9. One (1) Baby Blanket for Scene Four.
10. One (1) Baby Doll for Scene Four.

PRODUCTION NOTES

This particular biblical dramatization was created and performed for a liturgy in the Mission Church for the thirty-second Sunday in Ordinary Time. The readings, including Matthew 25:1-13, were from the Roman Catholic Lectionary, Cycle "A."

There are certain references that could use some explanation on my part and adaptation on your part. In Scene One there is a press conference held by the man who was President of the United States in the fall of 1988. You may wish to change the name of the president to that of the person who actually holds that office at the time you perform this biblical dramatization. The quote about homelessness, however, is an actual quote of President Reagan and might carry much more of an impact coming from his mouth. The young man who played the role of President Reagan did a commendable imitation of President Reagan's voice and head-bobbing.

The names of the Players who actually helped create and first perform this biblical dramatization are used in the script (e.g. Brennan, Ann, Jim, Christi, Matthew, etc.). One way that you can adapt this script is by using the names of the people with whom you are working. Some of the places, like the Hut, are local Santa Clara University students' hangouts. The Hut is a dingy-looking, dim-lit bar that has acquired mythical significance in the minds of Santa Clara students and the memories of some Santa Clara graduates. Since the Hut will have appropriately little or no significance for your audience or congregation, this would be another opportunity for you to adapt and change the script.

Alcohol and substance abuse is the focus of Scene Two. It is not only a problem on university campuses. There are dysfunctional family systems everywhere. This scene explores the nature of "codependency" or the ways that the network of relationships can unconsciously support disease through their denial of the existence of the problem. The potential consequences of such willful ignorance are disastrous as this scene dramatically demonstrates.

A few comments are in order about the subjects of the game show in Scene Three. While Santa Clara University has produced an honor roll of graduates who have gone on to make significant contributions to their respective communities, there is also a list of those who were not affected or significantly shaped by the Jesuit ideals or Judaeo-Christian values of the university. Ramon Meliam Rodriguez is a sober reminder to all of us about the wisdom and foolishness of our behaviors, our attitudes, our choices and our commitments.

Santa Clara University does not have a large fraternity and sorority population. The irresponsible behavior of some members of fraternities on the campus has unfortunately labeled the character of all of the Greek population. The event mentioned in this scene is one of many philanthropic activities undertaken by the men and women that belong to these organizations. It was used as a reminder and a challenge to "expand our vision" in our understanding and evaluation of these organizations and those who belong to them.

If any of the events or references are too local to be of significance for your audience or congregation, by all means change and adapt this script to meet your needs and purposes. These biblical dramas were created by the Biblical Explorers. This group of Santa Clara University students and staff met weekly in an effort to make "connections" between the reality of the biblical story and the reality of their life. The events that were happening around us shed light on the meaning of the scriptures. Conversely, the scriptures oftentimes illumined unexamined aspects of our daily experience. You and your reflection group are invited into this same process as you attempt to make your own "connections" with the scriptures and biblical dramatizations of this volume.

REFLECTION QUESTIONS AND EXERCISES

1. There are three parables or stories in the twenty-fifth chapter of Matthew's Gospel. They all deal with "wisdom" and "foolishness" in one way or another. I invite you and your reflection group to look at Matthew 25:31-46. Read it out loud three times. Pause between each reading of the parable so that people can have some time to reflect on the story. When you are ready, I invite you and your reflection group to consider some of the following questions.

What characters in this story would you and your reflection group characterize as "foolish"? Why do you think they are foolish? What characters in this story would you and your reflection group characterize as "wise"? Why do you think they are wise?

I invite you and your reflection group to think of other examples from the Bible and from life that demonstrate the wisdom or foolishness of people. What examples would your reflection group suggest? How and why does the behavior of these characters reveal an attitude of wisdom or foolishness? Explain.

For you and your reflection group, what are some examples of "foolish" attitudes? For you and your reflection group, what are some examples of "foolish" behavior? What characterizes "foolishness" in attitude and behavior for you and your reflection group? For you and your reflection group, what are some examples of "wise" attitudes? For you and your reflection group, what are some examples of "wise" behavior? What characterizes "wisdom" in attitude and behavior for you and your reflection group?

2. St. Ignatius of Loyola talks about "wise" and "foolish" attitudes and behaviors in the prologue to his *Spiritual Exercises.* In the "First Principle and Foundation," St. Ignatius points out that men and women were created "to praise, reverence and serve God" and by this means to save their souls. All the rest of creation has been given to men and women to assist them in attaining this end. To the extent that creation helps us to our end, our use of creatures demonstrates "wisdom." To the extent that creation ever frustrates our purpose or end, in those instances our use of creatures is "foolish" (*Spiritual Exercises,* No. 23).

I invite you and your reflection group to consider four aspects of creation that are part of any human life. Those four aspects are: (1) work, (2) play, (3) prayer, and (4) relationships.

What do you and your reflection group think would be "wise" attitudes and behaviors toward work? What do you think would be "foolish" attitudes toward work? How can work help us praise God? How can work help us show reverence for God? How can work help us serve God? Explain.

What do you and your reflection group think would be "wise" attitudes and behaviors toward play? What do you think would be "foolish" attitudes and behaviors toward play? How can play help us praise God? How can play help us show reverence for God? How can play help us serve God? Explain.

What do you and your reflection group think would be "wise" attitudes and behaviors toward prayer? What do you think would be "foolish" attitudes and behaviors toward prayer? How can prayer help us praise God? How can prayer help us show reverence for God? How can prayer help us serve God? Explain.

What do you and your reflection group think would be "wise" attitudes and behaviors toward relationships? What do you think would be "foolish" attitudes and behaviors toward relationships? How can relationships help us praise God? How can relationships help us show reverence for God? How can relationships help us serve God? Explain.

3. Meister Eckhart, a fourteenth century German mystic, has been rediscovered and once again brought to our attention through the work and writing of Matthew Fox. Meister Eckhart once defined "wisdom"

as the ability to do the next thing you have to do, the ability to do it with your whole heart, and the ability to take delight in doing it. I invite you and your reflection group to explore the challenge and invitation of Eckhart's definition through the following questions.

Do you and your reflection group think it is hard or easy to do the next thing you have to do? Explain. At what times in your life have you found it easy to do the next thing you have to do? What made it so easy for you? Explain. At what times in your life have you found it hard to do the next thing you had to do? What made it so difficult for you? Explain. Why do you think Meister Eckhart says that the ability to do the next thing you have to do demonstrates "wisdom"? Do you and your reflection group agree or disagree with this evaluation? Explain. What behaviors or attitudes would you have to change in your life in order to be better able to do the next thing you have to do? Explain.

Do you and your reflection group think it is difficult or easy to do things with your whole heart? Explain. At what times in your life have you found it easy to be wholehearted in what you were doing? What made it easy for you to be wholehearted? Explain. At what times in your life have you found it difficult to be wholehearted in what you were doing? What made it difficult for you to be wholehearted? Explain. Why do you think that Meister Eckhart says that the ability to be wholehearted in what you are doing demonstrates "wisdom"? Do you and your reflection group agree or disagree with this evaluation? Explain. What behaviors or attitudes would you have to change in your life in order to be more wholehearted in what you are doing?

Do you and your reflection group think it is difficult or easy to take delight in what you are doing? Explain. At what times in your life have you found it easy to take delight in what you were doing? What made it easy for you to take delight in what you were doing? Explain. At what times in your life did you find it difficult to take delight in what you were doing? What made it difficult for you to take delight in what you were doing? Explain. Why do you think Meister Eckhart says that the ability to take delight in what you are doing is a demonstration of "wisdom"? Explain. Do you and your reflection group agree or disagree with this evaluation? Explain. What behaviors or attitudes would you have to change in your life in order to take more delight in what you are doing? Explain.

4. Elie Wiesel, in an interview published in *America* magazine (November 19, 1988), was asked how he could continue to look for and find hope after the horrendous experience of the Holocaust. He said: "I find enough sources of despair by opening the newspapers every day, or listening to the news. Yet, at the same time, every day I find new sources for hope. Each time a person surprises me by remaining human, by offering a gift, being generous, resisting evil, and surely by fighting evil, I am grateful to God, grateful that I am a contemporary of that person. This is truly a reason for hope." Do you and your reflection group think this is a "wise" or "foolish" definition of hope? Explain.

What are some of the sources of despair that you have encountered through the newspapers you have read these past days and weeks? What was there about the news that evoked this response in you? What are some of the sources of despair that you have experienced by listening to the news on the radio or watching it on television? What was there about the news that evoked this response in you? What new sources of hope have you found in your life recently? Have you ever been surprised by a person remaining human in some situation or circumstance? Why would this be a cause for hope? Explain. Have you ever been surprised by a person offering you a gift? What shapes and forms do those gifts take? Why would this be a cause for hope? Explain. Have you ever been surprised by someone being generous in a situation? What shapes and forms did their generosity take? Why would this be a cause for hope? Have you ever been surprised by someone in your life resisting evil? What does it mean to resist evil? What are some of the evils we are challenged to resist in our culture and society today? Why would someone resisting evil be a cause for hope? Explain. Have you ever been surprised by someone in your life fighting evil? What does it mean to fight evil? What are some of the evils we are challenged to fight in our culture and society today? Why not consider poverty, hunger and homelessness for starters? How can you fight poverty in our culture and society? How can you fight hunger in our culture and society? How can you fight homelessness in our culture and society? Explain. Why would someone fighting evil be a cause for hope? Explain.

5. In the first scene of this biblical dramatization, what were the examples of foolishness from the history of the world? Why did Noah's neighbors think he was foolish? What did Noah reveal of his character through his actions or behavior? What did Noah's neighbors reveal of

their character through their actions or behavior? Why would the Captain of the Titanic be included as an example of foolishness in this dramatization? Do you agree or disagree with this evaluation of him? Do you and your reflection group think there are people in the United States who are homeless? If so, why? If not, why not? Explain. If you do think there are homeless people in the United States, what do you think of the President's comment that "There are no homeless in America"? Explain.

6. What do you and your reflection group discover about the character of Student-1 in Scene Two from her behavior and attitudes? Do you think she has a drinking problem? If so, why? If not, why not? Explain.

What do you and your reflection group discover about the character of Roomie-1 in Scene Two from her behavior and attitudes? Is her concern about Student-1's drinking problem warranted or unwarranted? Explain. Have you ever heard of the term "tough love"? What do you think "tough love" is? Does Roomie-1 reveal herself to be a true or fair-weather friend to Student-1 in Scene Two? How does she reveal this? Explain.

What do you and your reflection group discover about the character of the Parent in Scene Two from his behavior and attitudes? If you were the Parent and Roomie-1 came to you with concern about the potential drinking problem of your child, would you have behaved or acted any differently? If so, why? If not, why not? Explain.

What do you and your reflection group discover about the character of Student-2 and Student-3 in Scene Two from their behavior and attitudes? If you had been a passenger in that car, would you have allowed Student-1 to drive? If so, why? If not, why not? Explain.

Now I invite you and your reflection group to go back over Scene Two and discuss whether you think the behavior and attitudes of each character embody "wisdom" or "foolishness." What are your reasons for evaluating each character as "wise" or "foolish"?

7. In Scene Four of this biblical dramatization, who does Student-4 reveal herself to be through her actions and attitudes? Explain. In Scene Four of this biblical dramatization, who does Roomie-2 reveal himself to be through his actions and attitudes? Explain.

In Scene Four, Student-4 tells Roomie-2: "I want to know more about hunger. I'm afraid that what we don't know can kill people." Do you and your reflection group agree or disagree with her sentiments? Explain.

What do you and your reflection group know about the hungry in your town or city? What do you and your reflection group know about hunger? What statistics does Student-4 share with Roomie-2 about hunger in Scene Four? How do you and your reflection group react to these facts? What local organizations are there in your town or city that collect and distribute food to the hungry? I encourage you and your reflection group to take the time to discover more about the problem of hunger in your local community as well as the larger global community. If you don't know much about Oxfam International, write them for more information about what they do. Their address and phone number is listed in the reflection questions and exercises of the previous biblical drama. More educational resources on hunger are available through *Bread for the World,* 802 Rhode Island Ave., N.E., Washington, D.C. 20018. I think it would be particularly educational and helpful to discover what resources you have available through local civic or church food banks. Student-4 quotes the Chinese philosopher Lao-Tzu. What is one step that each of you can take on the journey toward understanding and responding to the problem of hunger in our world?

8. I invite you and your reflection group to create a cinquain (i.e. a five-line piece of poetry) on "wisdom" and another cinquain on "foolishness." For a description and explanation of the literary form of the cinquain, refer to reflection question 8 from the biblical drama *What Happens Next?* After you have written your cinquains on "wisdom" and "foolishness," share them with the other members of your reflection group. What new insights do you get into "wisdom" or "foolishness" from what you have written? Explain. What new insights do you get into "wisdom" or "foolishness" from what the other members of your reflection group have written? Explain.

5. The Last Judgment

(Matthew 25:31-46)

"When the Son of man comes in his glory, and all the angels with him, then he will sit on his glorious throne. Before him will be gathered all the nations, and he will separate them one from another as a shepherd separates the sheep from the goats, and he will place the sheep at his right hand, but the goats at the left. Then the King will say to those at his right hand, 'Come, O blessed of my Father, inherit the kingdom prepared for you from the foundation of the world; for I was hungry and you gave me food, I was thirsty and you gave me drink, I was a stranger and you welcomed me, I was naked and you clothed me, I was sick and you visited me, I was in prison and you came to me.' Then the righteous will answer him, 'Lord, when did we see thee hungry and feed thee, or thirsty and give thee drink? And when did we see thee a stranger and welcome thee, or naked and clothe thee? And when did we see thee sick or in prison and visit thee?' And the King will answer them, 'Truly, I say to you, as you did it to one of the least of these my brethren, you did it to me.' Then he will say to those at his left hand, 'Depart from me, you cursed, into the eternal fire prepared for the devil and his angels; for I was hungry and you gave me no food, I was thirsty and you gave me no drink, I was a stranger and you did not welcome me, naked and you did not clothe me, sick and in prison and you did not visit me.' Then they also will answer, 'Lord, when did we see thee hungry or thirsty or a stranger or naked or sick or in prison, and did not minister to thee?' Then he will answer them, 'Truly, I say to you, as you did it not to one of the least of these, you did it not to me.' And they will go away into eternal punishment, but the righteous into eternal life."

But When?

CAST

Visitor-1 (Eric)
Visitor-2 (David)
Visitor-3 (Ignacio)
Visitor-4
Visitor-5 (Tina)
Anxiety
Thought-2
Thought-3
Thought-4
Thought-5
Roomie-1
Counselor-1
Counselor-2
Teacher (Dr. Hendricks)

Student-1 (Michele)
Student-2 (Dave)
Student-3 (Frances)
Student-4 (Duchess)
Student-5 (Craig)
Student-6 (Chris)
Student-7 (Todd)
Student-8 (Anne)
Student-9
Roomie-2
Brother (Paul)
Parent
Friend
Coach

SCENE ONE

[NOTE:

This dramatization is based upon the scriptural story found in Matthew 25:31-46. It consists of five brief vignettes, each of which focus on one of five descriptions that captures those that belong to the faith community: (a) sharing our bread with the hungry, (b) sharing our drink with the thirsty, (c) clothing the naked, (d) welcoming those away from home, and (e) visiting those in prison. After each vignette is done in the sanctuary area, that group of dramatists will move to a different area of the congregation for the final part of the dramatization.]

[The Players for Scene One come out on the platform. Student-1 comes out toward the congregation, speaks her scriptural line, then goes back to her place on the platform and Scene One comes to life.]

STUDENT-1:

When I was hungry...

[Student-1 goes to the main acting area. There are two blocks there. She sits on one and is obviously frustrated by all of the study and things she has to do.]

ANXIETY:

Knock! Knock! Knock!

STUDENT-1:

Oh great, just what I need, a visitor when I have twenty thousand things to get done. Maybe if I pretend I'm not here...

ANXIETY:

[Anxiety comes onto the platform. Michele is obviously upset.]

"I hear you knocking but you can't come in...."Hi, Michele. It's me again!

STUDENT-1:

Oh no, not you!

ANXIETY:

Yep! Just when you thought things couldn't get worse, here's free-floating anxiety, at your service! What are you working on?

STUDENT-1:

I've got this thirty-page paper due tomorrow.

ANXIETY:

You never were good at papers, Michele. Besides, you started so late on it. Just thinking about it must really tire you out.

[Student-1 nods her head in assent.]

You know what you need? Some sleep.

STUDENT-1:

But I can't sleep, I've got too much to think about.

ANXIETY:

That's right, Michele. You've been so preoccupied with your paper that you haven't had time to think about that blind date your roommate got you for the boat dance. She's been waiting for the right moment to get even with you, Michele.

STUDENT-1:

I don't want to think about that.

ANXIETY:

You don't have to, Michele. Why not relax and have a drink? "Some drink to remember. Some drink to forget."

[Student-1 takes a bottle of beer and drinks from it. There is a knock on the door.]

STUDENT-1:

Come on in. The door's open!

[Visitor-1 walks in.]

Eric, what are you doing here?

VISITOR-1:

I'm sorry to bother you, Michele, but I just broke up with Amy. I really need to talk to someone.

ANXIETY:

Go ahead, Michele, you've got nothing better to do.

STUDENT-1:

Eric, I'd like to talk, but it's really bad timing. I'm sick. I've got two thirty-page term papers due and I'm taking five midterms tomorrow. Any other time, but not right now.

VISITOR-1:

Sure. I understand. Here. I think these are yours. I found them outside your door.

[Visitor-1 hands Student-1 two envelopes and leaves.]

ANXIETY:

Nice going, Michele. You'll never see him again. And I'm sure he believed all those excuses with that can of beer in your hand.

STUDENT-1:

[Student-1 picks up the phone bill and bank statement.]

Oh no!

ANXIETY:

What's that, Michele—your phone bill and your bank statement?

[Student-1 nods her head "yes."]

When you wrote the check for that last phone bill, Michele, you didn't have enough money in the bank. You know what that means. Bounce! Bounce! Bounce!

STUDENT-1:

What am I going to do?

ANXIETY:

What do we do when your check bounces? Let's go shopping!

[Michele grabs her coat and purse. Just as she goes to the door, the phone rings. Visitor-2 is standing upstage looking nerdy. Michele goes to answer the phone.]

I'll bet that's your blind date calling to confirm the big date.

STUDENT-1:

[She picks up the phone, looks at it and yells into it.]

No!

[Student-1 slams the phone down.]

ANXIETY:

You have this knack for botching up everything, Michele. You've raised it to a high art form! You're a real cosmic blunderer!

STUDENT-1:

[Student-1 puts her hands over her ears.]

Take a deep breath.

[Student-1 takes in a deep breath and slowly lets it out.]

Again.

[Student-1 takes in another deep breath and lets it out.]

And again.

[Student-1 takes in one more deep breath and slowly lets it out. Student-1 folds her hands and begins to pray.]

"Give us this day our daily bread...and deliver us from all evil...."

ANXIETY:

Stop that! Don't do that, Michele. That's cheating!

STUDENT-1:

[Student-1 continues praying with more strength.]

"...forgive us our sins as we forgive those who sin against us. Lead us not into temptation...."

ANXIETY:

All right, Michele, have it your way. I'm leaving. But you haven't seen the last of me by a long shot!

[The Players from Scene One freeze momentarily and then go to a place in the congregation and sit. The Players from Scene Two come up to the platform. When they are in position, Visitor-3 comes forward and speaks.]

SCENE TWO

VISITOR-3:

> When I was thirsty...

> [Visitor-3 goes to the center stage and opens a letter. He is obviously excited at the news it contains. He goes to Student-2.]

> Hey, Dave, I got my letter of acceptance from the Jesuit Volunteers!

STUDENT-2:

> Good for you, Ignacio!

THOUGHT-2:

> [Student-2's alter ego.]

> Big deal! I'm worried about graduating and finding a job. And you want me to be excited about your "good news"?

VISITOR-3:

> [Visitor-3 moves toward Frances.]

> Frances, I was accepted by the Jesuit Volunteers!

STUDENT-3:

> Nice going!

THOUGHT-3:

> [Student-3's alter ego.]

> I can't believe this Mexican was accepted and I wasn't!

VISITOR-3:

> [Visitor-3 moves to Student-4.]

> Duchess, I'm in the Jesuit Volunteer Corps next year!

STUDENT-4:

> Well, that's great!

THOUGHT-4:

> [Student-4's alter ego.]

Yeah, just great! Santa Clara's answer to Mother Teresa. What are you trying to prove?

VISITOR-**3**:

[Visitor-3 goes to Student-5.]

Hey, Craig, guess what? I was accepted by the Jesuit Volunteers!

STUDENT-**5**:

Congratulations, Ignacio. I'm really happy for you!

THOUGHT-**5**:

[Student-5's alter ego.]

Congratulations, Ignacio. I'm really happy for you!

[All the Players from Scene Two freeze momentarily and then move to another part of the congregation and sit. The Players from Scene Three come up to the platform, and when they are ready, Student-6 comes forward and speaks.]

SCENE THREE

STUDENT-**6**:

I was naked…

[Student-6 goes to the center stage where she is joined on two blocks by Roomie-1. They are studying. Student-6 is having a very hard time. She finally slams her book closed.]

I've had it! I can't take it anymore!

ROOMIE-**1**:

It's only a test, Chris. You've gotten through other ones. You'll get through this one!

STUDENT-**6**:

I just want it all to be over!

ROOMIE-**1**:

For crying out loud, Chris, you've only got two more weeks. Just hang in there!

STUDENT-6:

> I want it all to be over!

ROOMIE-1:

> You mean school?

STUDENT-6:

> I mean everything! What difference does it make?

ROOMIE-1:

> When you start stressing like this, Chris, I don't know what to do. But one thing I know is that I can't concentrate. I'm going to the library. Why not take a nap. Things will look differently when you've had a little rest.

[Roomie-1 leaves. The phone rings.]

STUDENT-6:

> Hello.

BROTHER:

> Hey, Chris, it's your big brother. How's it going?

STUDENT-6:

> Not so good, Paul.

BROTHER:

> What's wrong? Are you in the middle of midterms again?

STUDENT-6:

> It's not just that, Paul. It's everything. I just don't see any point in going on.

BROTHER:

> Listen, Chris, I felt the same way when I was going there. I wish I was closer so we could get together for a long chat.

STUDENT-6:

> So do I.

BROTHER:

> But I'm sure there's help right there on campus. I used the

counseling services on more than one occasion. Why don't you check them out. O.K.?

STUDENT-6:

O.K..

BROTHER:

Love you, Chris.

STUDENT-6:

I love you, too, Paul.

[Student-6 gets up and goes over to where Counselor-1 is sitting.]

COUNSELOR-1:

I see we have five minutes left. Chris, you were pretty quiet during our session today. What's that all about?

STUDENT-6:

It's all getting to be pretty overwhelming for me.

COUNSELOR-1:

"It," Chris? Why don't you name that "it"?

STUDENT-6:

If I could, I would. That's what's frustrating me.

COUNSELOR-1:

Why don't we start with that next time, Chris. I see our time is over for this afternoon.

[Student-6 gets up to leave. She walks over to a block that Visitor-2 is on.]

STUDENT-6:

Hey, what are you doing?

VISITOR-2:

Sitting on the roof. Is that O.K.?

STUDENT-6:

Yeah, but it's kind of dangerous. Do you always come up here?

VISITOR-2:

No, only when I want to "end it all."

STUDENT-6:

What?

VISITOR-2:

I'm waiting for the wind to shift. I'm afraid if I jumped off now the wind might throw me back into the building. And you see, I can't do anything right. I don't want to goof this up.

STUDENT-6:

Do you mind if I sit down?

VISITOR-2:

Go right ahead.

STUDENT-6:

So things are pretty bad?

[Visitor-2 nods his head "yes."]

How bad?

VISITOR-2:

I don't get along with my roommate. I'm awkward when I meet new people so I don't have many friends. I don't fit into the floor. Everyone else around here is a blond-haired, blue-eyed Ken or Barbie doll that knows the right music, wears the right clothes, says the right things. They're a bunch of clones that do everything right. But don't get me wrong. I'm not just a social disaster, I'm self-destructing academically as well.

STUDENT-6:

What do you mean?

VISITOR-2:

I am one of two people in a class of seventy who are flunking introduction to chemistry. And science is supposed to be my strong point!

STUDENT-**6**:

So you're the other one. I'm lost in that class, too. My name is Chris. What's your name?

VISITOR-**2**:

David. Hi, Chris.

[There is an awkward pause. They look at each other and then away. Student-6 looks down.]

STUDENT-**6**:

See that red car down there?

VISITOR-**2**:

That's my car. It's only got 20,000 miles on it.

STUDENT-**6**:

I hate to tell you this, David, but I think you're getting ticketed for parking illegally. You don't want a ticket on top of all of this, do you?

[They look at each other and laugh.]

VISITOR-**2**:

Want to help me find another parking spot?

STUDENT-**6**:

Yeah!

[The Players from Scene Three freeze momentarily and then move to another part of the congregation. The Players from Scene Four come up to the platform. When they are ready, Visitor-4 comes forward and speaks.]

SCENE FOUR

VISITOR-**4**:

When I was a stranger...

[Visitor-4 moves back stage and sits cross-legged on one of the boxes.]

STUDENT-7:

So, what was so important that I had to come over right away?

STUDENT-8:

I got some bad news today.

STUDENT-7:

Did you get your calculus exam back?

STUDENT-8:

No! I got the results of my physical exam back! I'm pregnant!

STUDENT-7:

You're what?

STUDENT-8:

I'm pregnant!

STUDENT-7:

You mean you weren't on the pill? Damn it, Anne, you should have been more careful!

STUDENT-8:

Well listen, Todd, you could have been more careful yourself!

[Student-7 and Student-8 freeze.]

VISITOR-4:

God, I would love to stretch. It's a good thing I'm not claustro-phobic. If I were, nine months in closed quarters could drive me wacko!

[Visitor-4 freezes.]

STUDENT-7:

You're right, Anne. I'm as responsible as you are. So, I want to do the right thing. I'll pay for an abortion.

STUDENT-8:

Who says I want an abortion?

STUDENT-7:

Be reasonable, Anne. Think this thing through. Are you prepared to drop out of school and have this child? Are you prepared to give up the chance to go to med school to raise it? I'm not!

[Student-7 and Student-8 freeze.]

VISITOR-4:

God, I wonder what it's like out there? Just be patient! Be patient! There's so much I want to see and hear and taste and smell and touch.

[Visitor-4 freezes.]

COUNSELOR-2:

It's not up to me, Anne, as your counselor, to make the decision for you. All I want to help you do is become aware of your options.

PARENT:

Your father and I think you were foolish to get yourself into this position. But we want you to know we are willing to help you in whatever way we can.

STUDENT-7:

Well, I don't know about you, but I don't want to bring one more unwanted human being into the world.

STUDENT-8:

I suppose that means you finally broke down and bought yourself some protection for the next time. Too bad you didn't think of that before!

FRIEND:

As your friend, Anne, I agree with you. You're not ready for marriage. But that's not the only alternative. You can drop out of school for a quarter. Have your baby and put it up for adoption. Isn't it ironic? There are people out there who desperately want a child and can't have one. You can have a baby and don't know if you want one.

[All the Players freeze except Visitor-4.]

VISITOR-4:

I wonder whether I'll be "sugar and spice and everything nice" or "snips and snails and puppy dog tails." There ought to be some way to tell.

[Visitor-4 looks as though he is taking a peek into his pants.]

Well, here's one for the puppy dog tails! I sure am curious. I wonder what my mom will be like? I wonder what my father will teach me? I wonder what I will become?

[Visitor-4 freezes.]

STUDENT-8:
Well, everyone seems to be an expert on what I should do!

COUNSELOR-2:
People mean well, Anne. They are just too full of advice at times. One thing is clear: this is an important decision and one that you must make.

[All the Players from Scene Four freeze momentarily and then move to another part of the congregation. The Players from Scene Five come up to the platform. When they are ready, Visitor-5 comes forward and speaks.]

SCENE FIVE

VISITOR-5:
When I was in prison…

[Visitor-5 goes to the middle of the stage. All of the other characters, except Roomie-2, are behind her in a semi-circular fashion.]

COACH:
You've missed two intramural games in a row, Tina. You're letting me down. You're letting your team down. And you're letting yourself down.

VISITOR-5:
I've been kinda busy. I'll try to be there next time.

COACH:
Try-ers are liars, Tina. Be there!

[Coach turns his back.]

STUDENT-9:

Tina, when you signed up for S.P.A.C.E. you knew it was going to mean a lot of work.

VISITOR-5:

I just didn't know it would take so much time.

STUDENT-9:

As publicity coordinator you've got to stay on top of things, Tina. Attendance is down at our events and I think that's due, in large part, to you.

VISITOR-5:

I'm trying.

STUDENT-9:

Well, try harder. You've got to advertise events if you want attendance. Here are some flyers I want you to post for the upcoming rafting trip. O.K.?

VISITOR-5:

O.K.

[Student-9 turns around as Roomie-2 comes in.]

ROOMIE-2:

Have you had anything to eat yet?

VISITOR-5:

No.

ROOMIE-2:

Why don't you take a little break and join us for a piece of pizza next door?

VISITOR-5:

I'd love to but I've got a few errands to run. Plus I'm expecting a phone call from my English teacher. How about saving me a piece? I'll be over in a bit.

[Roomie-2 leaves.]

TEACHER:

Miss Johnson, how do you define late? Webster's New World Dictionary defines it this way: "happening or coming after the usual or expected time." That describes your term paper, Tina.

VISITOR-5:

I know, Dr. Hendricks, but I've had so much to do that I'm running a little bit behind. If you'll just give me some more time.

TEACHER:

I gave you an extension on your outline. You had better start getting your priorities straightened out, Tina, if you expect to stay in this university.

[Teacher turns around as Roomie-2 comes back in.]

ROOMIE-2:

It's getting late, kiddo. You know what you need? Some food and a little rest.

VISITOR-5:

But I've got this stuff to do for S.P.A.C.E. and my term paper is already overdue. And if I don't get them done tomorrow, I'll never be able to make it to the intramural football game.

ROOMIE-2:

It doesn't sound as if you want to do all those things, Tina. What do you want?

[There's a pause as Visitor-5 and Roomie-2 look at each other.]

VISITOR-5:

What do I want? I want some time for myself. I want to be able to curl up and take a long nap and not feel guilty about it. I want to read a good book that doesn't have anything to do with one of my classes. I want to walk in the rain. I want to be able to sit down and talk to a good friend and not squeeze it in between the fifty other things I'm supposed to do. I want some cut flowers.

[The awareness Visitor-5 discovers in these last lines leads her to begin crying. Roomie-2 gives her a big hug.]

ROOMIE-2:

Say, do you hear that? I think it's starting to rain.

SCENE SIX

SCENE-1:

> [All The Players in Scene One stand.]

> But when did we see you hungry and give you something to eat?

SCENE-2:

> [All the Players in Scene Two stand.]

> When did we see you thirsty and give you something to drink?

SCENE-3:

> [All the Players in Scene Three stand.]

> When did we see you naked and clothe you?

SCENE-4:

> [All the Players in Scene Four stand.]

> Away from home and welcome you?

SCENE-5:

> [All the Players in Scene Five stand.]

> In prison and visit you?

VISITOR-1:

> When you did it ...

VISITOR-3:

> ...to the least ...

STUDENT-6:

> ...of your brothers or sisters...

VISITOR-4:

> ...know that you did it...

VISITOR-5:

> ...to me.

—FINIS—

PROPS

1. Two (2) Bar Stools which will be used in Scene One and later in Scene Four.
2. Two (2) Books which will be used in Scene One and Scene Three.
3. Assorted Papers which will be used in Scene One.
4. One (1) Bottle of Beer. Empty the beer bottle and replace its contents with ginger ale or root beer which will give the impression of being beer.
5. Two (2) Envelopes for use in the First Scene. One is a bank statement and the other is a phone bill.
6. One (1) Letter for use in Scene Two.
7. Two (2) general purpose wooden theater blocks. These are often found in theater rehearsal halls. They are sturdy wooden oblong box shapes that can be used as seats or other props in dramas. Substitute something appropriate if you do not have access to these props.
8. Two (2) Phones for use in Scene Three.

PRODUCTION NOTES

This particular biblical drama is based on Matthew 25:31-46. This Gospel is part of the liturgy for the feast of Christ the King, Cycle "A."

The acronym S.P.A.C.E. is used in Scene Five. This refers to a campus organization at Santa Clara University called *Students Programming Alternate Campus Events.* This is one obvious place where the particular reference would have no significance for your study group or worship community. Therefore, adaptation is not only appropriate but necessary. Use this as a general principle throughout these biblical dramas.

REFLECTION QUESTIONS AND EXERCISES

1. I invite you and your reflection group to read over the biblical story from the twenty-fifth chapter of Matthew's Gospel three times. Have a member of your reflection group read it out loud each time. Pause between each reading of the text (Mt 25:31-46) so that the members of your group have a chance to reflect on the story. When you are ready to proceed, share together on the following questions.

What do you and your reflection group think Jesus means by "when I was hungry you fed me"? What are the ways that we feed people when they are hungry? Take this literally and figuratively. What are people hungry for? What are you hungry for? What will satisfy their hunger? What will satisfy your hunger? Explain. What are some of the ways we fail to feed people when they are hungry? Explain.

What do you and your reflection group think Jesus means by the phrase "when I was thirsty you gave me drink"? What are the ways that we give drink to the thirsty? What do people thirst for? What do you thirst for? What will satisfy their thirst? What will satisfy your thirst? Explain. What are some of the ways we fail to quench people's thirst? Explain.

What do you and your reflection group think Jesus means by "when I was a stranger you welcomed me"? What are the ways we welcome the stranger? What makes people feel strange? What makes you feel strange? What makes people feel welcome? What makes you feel welcome? Explain. What are some of the ways that we consciously or unconsciously fail to welcome strangers? Explain.

What do you and your reflection group think Jesus means by "when I was naked you clothed me"? What are some of the ways we can clothe the naked? What makes people feel naked? What makes you feel naked? How might someone clothe his/her nakedness? How might someone clothe your nakedness? Explain. What are some of the ways that we consciously or unconsciously fail to clothe the naked? Explain.

What do you and your reflection group think Jesus means by "when I was sick you visited me"? What are some of the ways we visit the sick? What are some of the ways we consciously or unconsciously fail to visit the sick. Explain.

What do you and your reflection group think Jesus means by "when I was in prison you went to see me"? What does it mean to be in prison? What are some of the ways we can go to see those in prison? What might this entail? Explain. What are some of the ways we consciously or unconsciously fail to go and see those in prison? Explain. If we don't visit those in prison, what do you think it might be that we don't want to see? Explain.

Why do you and your reflection group think Jesus blesses the one group and curses the other group? Which group would you find yourself in today? Explain. Having reflected on this story, are there any changes you would like to make in your attitudes and behaviors? If so, why? If not, why not? Explain.

2. Have you ever hungered for someone to hear you out? How would you describe the people who have been able to listen to you? Have you ever been able to listen to someone who was hungry for another person to hear him/her out? Why or why not? Have you ever thirsted for a word that would satisfy? Have you ever wished people would speak the truth? Have you ever wished they would speak to you from the heart? Have you ever been able to do this for others? Why or why not? When you have been hurting, naked, and most vulnerable, have you ever wished that people could touch you in a healing way? Have you ever been able to offer this healing touch to those who are hurt or vulnerable around you? Why or why not? When you have felt as if you were in prison, has anyone ever broken through the walls that divide you and isolate you and gently brought you into community? Have you ever been able to do this for others? Why or why not? When you have felt most alone, has anyone ever offered you true companionship? Have you ever been able to offer this to others? Why or why not?

3. St. Ignatius of Loyola, in his classic spiritual work *The Spiritual Exercises,* suggests a way of praying or contemplating biblical stories. He invites people to imaginatively place themselves within the biblical scene (no. 114-117). I suggest that you do this exercise in two different ways. First, do it as one of those who are called "blessed." See Christ on the throne. What does he communicate to you from his facial expressions and body language? What does he communicate with his tone of voice? Who are the other people with you who are being called "blessed" by Jesus? How does Christ's word strike you? Why are you so surprised when Jesus describes you as "blessed." What prayer would you like to pray to Jesus as a result of this experience?

The second time through, do it as one of those who are called "cursed." See Christ on the throne. What does he communicate through his facial expressions and body language? What does he communicate to you with the tone of voice that he uses? Who are the other people with you who are being called "cursed" by Jesus? What is your reaction to Jesus describing you as "cursed"? How would you respond to Jesus' evaluation of your failure to respond to the concrete needs around you? Why are you and the others surprised when Jesus describes you as "cursed"? What prayer would you like to pray to Jesus as a result of this experience?

4. John Donahue, S.J., in his book *The Gospel in Parable* (Philadelphia: Fortress Press, 1988), describes this section of Matthew's Gospel as an apocalyptic parable. What does "apocalyptic" mean? In both this parable from Matthew and Luke's parable about the Rich Man and Lazarus (Lk 16:19-31) "the time for conversion and change is past; what has been done on earth determines eternal destiny" (Donahue, p. 112). In many ways the parables shock us into examining whether and how much of our faith finds expression in the actions of our life. Imagine yourself as one of those who are called "blessed" in this scene. What advice would you give to your family and friends that might help them in the concrete everyday living of their faith? If you were allowed to give them five pieces of wisdom, what would those five pieces of wisdom be? How and why did you choose these five pieces of wisdom? Explain.

Now imagine yourself as one of those who are called "cursed" in this scene. If you could, what would you change in the living of your faith? What types of changes or conversion would you advise your family and friends to make? If you were allowed to give them five pieces of wisdom to assist them in the living out of their faith, what would those five pieces of wisdom be? How and why did you choose these five pieces of wisdom? Explain.

5. This parable contains six of the seven corporal works of mercy (to feed the hungry, to give drink to the thirsty, to clothe the naked, to shelter the homeless, to visit the imprisoned, to visit the sick, to bury the dead) which are part of the Christian tradition. What relationship do you and your reflection group find between these works of mercy and Christian discipleship? Explain. In the story drama, what do you and your reflection group think is the relationship between the particular work of mercy mentioned (e.g. "When I was hungry…") and the vignette that follows? Discuss and explain.

6. John Donahue believes that the ethic proposed in this parable of Matthew is an "ethics of discipleship" (p. 124). Through this parable we are once again invited to pattern our lives of faith on that of Jesus. Through this parable we are "to hear again the call 'Follow me' and are to be caught up in the mission of Jesus" (p. 125). What convincing evidence can you and your reflection group uncover about how Jesus lived what he preached? Where in the Gospels did Jesus literally or figuratively feed the hungry? Where in the Gospels did Jesus literally or figuratively give

drink to the thirsty? Where in the Gospels did Jesus literally or figuratively clothe the naked? Where in the Gospels did Jesus literally or figuratively shelter the homeless? Where in the Gospels did Jesus literally or figuratively minister to those in prison? Where in the Gospels did Jesus literally or figuratively visit the sick? Where in the Gospels did Jesus literally or figuratively bury the dead?

Donahue also believes that "no Gospel is harsher than Matthew on an ethics of words without deeds" (p. 125). To what forms of conversion does this parable call you and your reflection group? Discuss and explain. To what forms of conversion does this parable call our Christian communities? Discuss and explain. Who are some of the groups of people in our church and our society who experience neither justice nor mercy from us? Can we continue to deny these men and women, these incarnations of Christ's presence in our world today, the justice and mercy that living out the Gospel demands and still call ourselves Christian? If so, why? If not, why not? What are some examples of the ways that our behaviors and actions don't correspond or support the articulation of our faith? Explain. How can we change this? Discuss and explain.

7. In a prayer-poem entitled "Simple Things" from *God of Untold Tales* by Michael E. Moynahan, S.J. (San Jose: Resource Publications, 1979), the author suggests that God comes to us in three simple human experiences: interruptions, longings and waitings. Have your group read and reflect on this prayer-poem. What do you and your reflection group think the author means by saying that God comes to us in waitings? Explain. How does God come to you in your experiences of waiting? Explain. What prevents you from responding to the presence of God in waiting? Explain.

What do you and your reflection group think the author means by saying that God comes to us in hungers or longings? Explain. How does God come to you in your human experiences of hungering and longing? Explain. What might prevent you from meeting and responding to the presence of God that is found in the human experiences of hungering and longing? Explain.

What do you and your reflection group think the author means by saying that God comes to us in interruptions? Explain. What have been some of the major and minor interruptions of your life? Does illness interrupt your "normal" life? Does the death of parents, relatives or loved ones interrupt your life? Do the homeless occasionally interrupt your life? How? Do the cries of the poor interrupt your life? If so, why? If not, why not? How does God come to you in the human experiences of interruptions? Explain. What might prevent you from meeting or responding to the presence of God that finds expression in the human experience of being interrupted? Explain.

8. I invite you and your reflection group to write a cinquain on: (1) the hungry, (2) the thirsty, (3) the stranger, (4) the naked, (5) the sick, and (6) those imprisoned. If you are not familiar with the literary form of the cinquain, refer to reflection question 8 from the biblical drama *What Happens Next?* You might have a couple of people in your reflection group write on one of the six different groups in need. When you have finished writing these cinquains, have the people share them. What have you learned about the hungry through these cinquains? What have you learned about the thirsty through these cinquains? What have you learned about the strangers in our society and community through these cinquains? What have you learned about those who are naked through these cinquains? What have you learned about the sick through these cinquains? What have you learned about those in prison through these cinquains?

6. The Barren Fig Tree

(Luke 13:1-9)

There were some present at that very time who told him of the Galileans whose blood Pilate had mingled with their sacrifices. And he answered them, "Do you think that these Galileans were worse sinners than all the other Galileans, because they suffered thus? I tell you, No; but unless you repent you will all likewise perish. Or those eighteen upon whom the tower in Siloam fell and killed them, do you think that they were worse offenders than all the

119

others who dwelt in Jerusalem? I tell you, No; but unless you repent you will all likewise perish." And he told this parable: "A man had a fig tree planted in his vineyard; and he came seeking fruit on it and found none. And he said to the vinedresser, 'Lo, these three years I have come seeking fruit on this fig tree, and I find none. Cut it down; why should it use up the ground?' And he answered him, 'Let it alone, sir, this year also, till I dig about it and put on manure. And if it bears fruit next year, well and good; but if not, you can cut it down.'"

Change Your Ways

CAST

Host-1

Passenger-1 (Steve)

Passenger-2 (Joe)

Woman-1

Woman-2

Host-2 (Laura)

Husband-1 (Chris)

Husband-2 (Garth)

Wife-1 (Tarie)

Wife-2 (Cari)

Person-5

Person-7

Player-1 (Tina)

Player-2 (Matthew)

Player-3 (Anne)

Player-4 (Ignacio)

Player-5 (Christi)

Player-6 (John)

Person-1

Person-2

Person-3

Person-4

Person-6

SCENE ONE

HOST-1:

All right, contestants, it's time to play "Name That Phobia!" [This
is yelled out by the players on both teams.] Our contestants come
from Santa Clara University and the University of California,
Berkeley. The game consists of two rounds. In round one I will
give you the name of the phobia and you must tell me what it
means. In round two I will give you clues about the particular

phobia and you must give me its proper name. Remember, only hit your buzzer when you know the answer. Please be as precise as possible when naming this evening's selected phobias. I see everyone is ready to play, so let's begin. Players, what is xenophobia? [Tina hits her buzzer.] Tina, SCU.

PLAYER-1:

A fear of Eastern forms of prayer.

HOST-1:

No. Can you take it, Cal Berkeley? [Player-4 hits his buzzer.] Ignacio, Cal Berkeley.

PLAYER-4:

Xenophobia is a fear of the foreigner or the stranger.

HOST-1:

That's right. Next question: What is curvaphobia? [Player-2 hits his buzzer.] Matthew, SCU.

PLAYER-2:

Curvaphobia is a fear of bodacious women.

HOST-1:

Imaginative, Matthew, but wrong. [Player-5 hits her buzzer.] Christi, Cal Berkeley.

PLAYER-5:

Curvaphobia is a fear that there will be ten Asians in your calculus class who will wreck the grading curve.

HOST-1:

Right again, Cal Berkeley. Here's the next question: What is graffitaphobia? [Player-3 hits her buzzer.] Anne, SCU.

PLAYER-3:

Graffitaphobia is a fear of seeing your name written in a bathroom.

HOST-1:

Wrong, Anne, but if it's any consolation, you're on the right track. Can you take it, Cal Berkeley? [Player-6 hits his buzzer.] John.

PLAYER-6:

Graffitaphobia is a fear of finding racist remarks written on bulletin boards or in public rest rooms.

HOST-1:

That's absolutely right. [Horn sounds.] Well, that's the end of round one. Our returning champions have sixty points while our challengers aren't on the scoreboard. But things could change in round two. Now I will give you clues and it's your turn to "Name That Phobia." Here's your first chance. You might have demonstrated this fear before you got to college. It would have surfaced when you put down your preference for the type of person you wanted to share a room with when you got to college. [Player-1 hits her buzzer.] Tina, SCU.

PLAYER-1:

What is Swigaphobia?

HOST-1:

Sorry, Tina. Cal Berkeley, here is your final clue. It is a fear of having a roommate who is a person of color. [Player-6 hits his buzzer.] John, I thought you might have an idea about this. Your answer please.

PLAYER-6:

What is roomataphobia?

HOST-1:

That's right, John. Here's your next set of clues. This fear has to do with who you might invite to a movie or a dance. [Player-2 hits his buzzer.] Matthew, SCU.

PLAYER-2:

·What is scagaphobia?

HOST-1:

I'm sorry, Matthew, that is incorrect. Cal Berkeley, here's your final clue. It is a fear of going on a date with someone who has a different ethnic background than yours. [Player-4 hits his buzzer.] Ignacio, Cal Berkeley.

PLAYER-4:

What is dataphobia?

HOST-1:

Correct. All right, SCU, here's your last chance to get on the board. [Anne hits her buzzer.] Anne, SCU.

PLAYER-3:

What is failaphobia?

HOST-1:

No, Anne. I won't count that. Please listen first for the clues. If fear and ignorance are the roots of diseases such as racism and sexism, this is a fear of the antidote. If the scripture writer is correct that "the truth will make you free," this is a fear of the truth. [Player-5 hits her buzzer.] Christi, Cal Berkeley.

PLAYER-5:

What is veraphobia? [All the characters freeze.]

HOST-1:

Change your ways...

PLAYERS:

[Together]...or we will all perish.

SCENE TWO

PASSENGER-1:

With our luck there probably won't be a seat on the train.

PASSENGER-2:

I don't care where you store it, but get rid of that negative karma. [They find two seats in the back of the train.] How wrong you are, you pessimist!

PASSENGER-1:

I just hope we make it on time for the Martin Luther King celebration.

PASSENGER-2:

Relax, Steve, we have plenty of time. [Joe looks at Steve who is visibly nervous.] What's wrong with you, Steve? Are you afraid Yasir Arafat is on this train?

PASSENGER-1:

I'm a little nervous about it being so late at night…on the train …and we're headed for a bad part of town.…You never know what might happen to you down here. [Three young women get on the train.]

PASSENGER-2:

Hey, look at those three black chicks. Now they are bad!

PASSENGER-1:

Do you think they've got a gun in that purse?

PASSENGER-2:

Steve, I wasn't referring to their character. I meant I find them irresistibly attractive.

PASSENGER-1:

[Ignoring what Joe has said.] Maybe they have a knife in there.

PASSENGER-2:

It's probably just makeup, Steve. [The three women start moving toward them.]

PASSENGER-1:

They're coming toward us. What are we going to do?

WOMAN-1:

Do you guys have the time?

PASSENGER-2:

Sure. Here, you can have my watch.

PASSENGER-1:

You can have my watch too. You never know when you may need an extra one.

WOMAN-1:

But I don't want your watches.

PASSENGER-1:

> [With a lightning bolt of insight he looks at Steve.] Keys!

PASSENGER-2:

> Yes, of course, keys. Here. Take the keys to my car.

WOMAN-1:

> But I don't want your car.

PASSENGER-1:

> [Panicking now as he tries to figure out what the women really want.] Of course, why didn't I think of it to begin with. [He gestures to Steve as he gets his wallet.]

PASSENGER-2:

> Here, take our money.

WOMAN-1:

> But I don't want your money.

PASSENGER-2:

> Tell us what you want, ladies, and we'll give it to you.

PASSENGER-1:

> Just don't hurt us. Please, don't hurt us.

WOMAN-1:

> Forget it, man. All we really wanted was the time. [All the characters freeze.]

WOMEN:

> [Together.] Change your ways...or we will all perish.

SCENE THREE

HOST-2:

> [The Players begin humming the theme from The Newlywed Game show.] Welcome everyone to a special edition of The Newlywed Game. Our contestants this evening come from Santa Clara University. Couple number one, Chris and Tarie, how long have you been married?

HUSBAND-1:

Six months.

WIFE-1:

And five days.

HOST-2:

And couple number two, Garth and Cari, how long have you two lovebirds been living in the nest together?

HUSBAND-2:

[Somewhat embarrassed.] Well, Laura, Cari and I were living together before we got…[Cari cuts Garth off.]

WIFE-2:

We've been married one year, Laura.

HOST-2:

O.K., husbands, if you'll leave for a moment, we'll ask you wives some questions and see how well they know you. [The husbands leave the stage and freeze with backs to congregation and fingers in their ears.] Now, ladies, what are most men looking for in a relationship? Tarie?

WIFE-1:

I think Chris will say, "Anything they can get."

HOST-2:

Cari, what do you think Garth will say?

WIFE-2:

"Someone who looks good on their arm."

HOST-2:

Question number two for you, ladies. Why don't men ask women out for a date on Santa Clara's campus? Cari?

WIFE-2:

They much prefer getting wasted.

HOST-2:

Tarie?

WIFE-1:

They're too macho.

HOST-2:

O.K., let's call the men back in. [The men come running back in and take their respective seats.] Now, men, we asked your wives this question: "What are most men looking for in a relationship?" Chris, what do you think Tarie said you would say?

HUSBAND-1:

Commitment.

HOST-2:

Well, Chris, what Tarie thought you would say was "Anything they can get." [Chris and Tarie communicate their disagreement verbally. Host-2 finally steps in.] And Garth, what do you think Cari said you would say?

HUSBAND-2:

Probably, someone who listens and really understands.

HOST-2:

She thought you'd say, "Someone who looks good on their arm." [Garth and Cari exchange words of dismay.] All right, fellas, here's your next question. Why don't men ask women out for a date on Santa Clara's campus? Chris?

HUSBAND-1:

They're afraid of being rejected.

HOST-2:

And Tarie guessed you would say: "They're too macho." [Chris and Tarie disagree verbally. Host-2 continues.] Garth, what do you think?

HUSBAND-2:

I'd say they're basically shy and afraid to risk.

HOST-2:

And Cari thought you would say: "They much prefer getting wasted." [A brief argument ensues here.] All right, wives, we'll see if your husbands can guess your responses better than you did theirs.

[The wives leave the stage area and have backs to the congregation with their fingers in their ears.] Men, what do you think most women are looking for at Santa Clara? Chris?

HUSBAND-1:

An "MRS." degree.

HOST-2:

Garth?

HUSBAND-2:

Trying to outdo the guys.

HOST-2:

And question number two: When you think of women athletes at Santa Clara University, what's your first impression? Chris?

HUSBAND-1:

They're all sexually frustrated. They're lesbians.

HOST-2:

Garth?

HUSBAND-2:

They're unhealthy competitors. They're trying to prove themselves.

HOST-2:

O.K., ladies, come back in here. [The women take their seats.] Ladies, why are most women at Santa Clara? Tarie?

WIFE-1:

To get a good education.

HOST-2:

That's a good response, Tarie, but Chris thought you would say: "To get a MRS. degree." [Chris and Tarie squabble verbally.] Cari, why do you think most women are at Santa Clara?

WIFE-2:

To develop an appreciation for and learn from differences.

HOST-2:

Well Garth thought you would say: "To outdo the guys." [Garth and Cari squabble verbally.] Ladies, here's our final question. When you think of women athletes at SCU, what's your first impression? Cari?

WIFE-2:

They achieve excellence in athletics, academics and other commitments.

HOST-2:

Well Garth predicted you'd say: "They're trying to prove themselves." [Cari and Garth bicker verbally.] Tarie, what's your response?

WIFE-1:

They throw themselves 100% into what they do.

HOST-2:

Another good response, but Chris thought you'd say: "They're all lesbians." [Chris and Tarie bicker verbally. Both couples go at it and finally freeze. The host looks at the congregation and says:]

Change your ways…or we will all perish.

SCENE FOUR

[This scene begins with six people wearing chains on their wrists. They have their backs to the congregation. As each one speaks, he/she turns around and moves out to a different part of the congregation. Underneath this entire scene can be heard the words of "The Battle Hymn of the Republic." It comes up loudly when the last person has proclaimed words from Dr. Martin Luther King, Jr.]

PERSON-1:

My name is Broken Promise. The land you are living on belonged to my ancestors. We had the wisdom you needed to live in peace with the environment. Yet you disrupted our families, our life, and our traditions. We were willing to live together but fear and greed drove you to herd us onto desolate pieces of land called reservations.

PERSON-2:

Most of your ancestors came to this country seeking freedom. My people were brought here against their will. We were sold as slaves and treated as property. In certain states we were not allowed to attend the same schools or churches that white people went to. We could not drink from the same water fountains, or ride in the same parts of public transportation. To this day our physical gifts tend to be admired while our intellectual gifts easily go unnoticed.

PERSON-3:

A potato famine brought me here. I came from a country proud of its national and religious traditions. I was looking only for a job and the opportunity to provide for those I loved. Imagine my sadness when I read your want ads and saw these words after most job listings: "Irish and Catholics Need Not Apply."

PERSON-4:

You let me into your country in the early 1800's when you needed cheap labor to build a railroad connecting your East and West coasts. You excluded me from your schools. You even made laws that prevented my people from coming to this country. As a result of continued riots and persecution the majority of my people were driven out of rural areas and into major Chinatowns to seek protection. This began the ghettos, the Chinatowns of the 20th century.

PERSON-5:

During the second world war my people, who had been here for over two generations, were gathered up by you and placed in internment camps. We lost our jobs and homes. When our loyalty was questioned, and that of our Italian and German brothers and sisters was not, we lost a great deal more. You robbed us of our rights and our dignity.

PERSON-6:

We are, geographically, neighbors. My people, too, have helped your agriculture business grow. For many years we provided cheap labor at harvest time. We long for the chance to share the opportunity and plenty of your country. You call us "illegal aliens" and construct fences and check points to keep us out. And when we are allowed in, you pass language laws that deprive us and our children of the education that could lead us to better jobs and greater financial security.

PERSON-7:

[All the characters freeze.] Change your ways...

PERSONS:

[Together]...or we will all perish.

PERSON-7:

[Stands on the small platform. He recites selections from Martin Luther King, Jr.'s "I Have a Dream" speech.]

PERSON-1:

I say to you today, my friends, even though we face the difficulties of today and tomorrow, I still have a dream. It is a dream deeply rooted in the American dream.

PERSON-6:

I have a dream that one day this nation will rise up and live out the true meaning of its creed: "We hold these truths to be self-evident: that all people are created equal."

PERSON-2:

I have a dream that my four little children will one day live in a nation where they will not be judged by the color of their skin but by the content of their character.

PERSON-5:

And if America is to be a great nation this must become true. So let freedom ring from the mighty mountains of New York.

PERSON-3:

Let freedom ring from the curvaceous slopes of California!

PERSON-4:

Let freedom ring from every hill and molehill of Mississippi. From every mountainside, let freedom ring.

PERSON-7:

And when this happens, and when we allow freedom to ring, when we let it ring from every village and every hamlet, from

every state and every city, we will be able to speed up that day
when all of God's children, black and white, Jews and Gentiles,
Protestants and Catholics, will be able to join hands and sing in
the words of that old Negro spiritual,

ALL:

"Free at last! Free at last! Thank God Almighty, we are free at
last!" [The characters freeze. "The Battle Hymn of the Republic"
gets louder. The lights gradually dim.]

—FINIS—

PROPS

1. One (1) Purse or Handbag.
2. Two (2) Wrist Watches.
3. One (1) Set of Keys.
4. Two (2) Wallets.
5. Seven (7) Pairs of Plastic Lengths of Chain or Colored Pieces of
   Thick Yarn worn around the wrists of the characters in Scene Four.
6. One (1) Recording of "The Battle Hymn of the Republic."
7. One (1) Small Box or Platform on which Person-7 can stand.

PRODUCTION NOTES

This biblical drama was based on Luke 13:1-9, the Gospel for the
third Sunday of Lent, Cycle "C." A number of experiences came
together to help shed light on the meaning and significance of the parable of the barren fig tree for the Biblical Explorers.

The first experiential influence was the celebration of the Martin
Luther King, Jr. holiday during our weeks of exploration with this
parable. The second experiential influence was a month-long celebration in February of the richness that different ethnic groups on
campus brought to the Santa Clara University community. The third
experiential influence was the focus on "conversion" during our
lenten observance. All three of these influences shaped the bridge
that we built between the Word of God and the experiences of our
life.

Scene One attempts to deal with some of the prejudices that students found present on the Santa Clara campus. While some of the phobias mentioned have imaginative rather than clinical status, each of them dealt with a very real instance of prejudice and intolerance by some Santa Clara students at that time. I encourage you and your study group to brainstorm and creatively examine some of the phobias that your community exhibits.

The Cal Berkeley team in Scene One that came up with the correct answers was composed of students who represented different ethnic backgrounds. The Santa Clara team of students were all Caucasian which reflected the make-up of the majority of the student body at that time. While the topic of prejudice is a very sensitive and serious one, I attempted to humorously get the congregation to both look at and laugh at some of the ridiculous things we fear.

"Hitting the buzzer" by the different team members in Scene One was accomplished by the particular student hitting the top of the bar stool with his/her hand and making a loud audible buzzer noise. I didn't list bar stools in the "props" because you don't need them. You can simply mime slamming your hand down on an imaginary buzzer and make the attendant buzzer sound.

Please keep in mind that you should adapt these biblical dramas to your own community needs. You might be better served to simply do one or two scenes rather than all four.

REFLECTION QUESTIONS AND EXERCISES

1. Lent, Holy Week culminating with the Sacred Triduum, and Easter are a time for the faith community to examine and renew their baptismal identity, their baptismal commitment and their baptismal mission. (See *Passage to the Paschal Feast: Weeks of Lent "C"* produced by The Liturgical Conference, 8750 Georgia Ave., Suite 123, Silver Spring, MD 20910-3621.) What do you and your group think our baptismal identity is? What do you and your group think our baptismal commitment is? What do you and your group think our baptismal mission is? How is Lent, Holy Week and Easter a time to examine and renew this baptismal identity, commitment and mission? How and why is it healthy and advisable to engage in such examination and renewal annually? Discuss and share.

2. One commentator on Luke's Gospel (Robert J. Karris, OFM in *The New Jerome Biblical Commentary,* p. 705) describes the parable of the barren fig tree as a parable of compassion and a parable of crisis. What do you and your study group find in this parable of Jesus that embodies or communicates compassion? Discuss and share. How do Jesus' words and actions demonstrate or communicate compassion? In what ways might this parable comfort the disciple who stumbles trying to follow the Christian Way? Discuss and share. What do you and your study group find in this parable of the fig tree that might make it a parable of crisis? Discuss and share. How do Jesus' words and actions demonstrate or communicate a crisis? Have each member of your study group consider some of the ways that he/she procrastinates in responding to Jesus' invitation to be his disciple. Have each member of your study group consider some of the ways that he/she is unproductive as a disciple of Jesus. Discuss and share. In what ways might this parable "light a fire under procrastinators and other unproductive disciples"? Discuss and share.

3. St. Ignatius of Loyola, in his *Spiritual Exercises,* has a meditation at the beginning of the Second Week entitled "The Call of Christ the King." In the second part of the meditation, Christ makes this appeal to us: "It is my will to win over the whole world, to conquer sin, hatred, and death—all the enemies between mankind and God. Whoever wishes to join me in this mission must be willing to labor with me, so that by following me in suffering, he may follow me in glory." (Contemporary translation by David L. Fleming from *The Spiritual Exercises of St. Ignatius: A Literal Translation and a Contemporary Reading.* St. Louis, MO: The Institute of Jesuit Sources, 1978.)

The word sin comes from the Greek *hamartia* which literally means "to miss the mark." What are some of the ways that you and your study group "miss the mark" in being disciples of Jesus? What are some of the different shapes that hatred takes? What are some of the different shapes that *prejudice* and *intolerance* take in our society? What are ways of thinking or feeling or acting that kill compassion, tolerance, hope, respect for all of creation, creativity, childlikeness, vision or dreams in ourselves and others? How are all of these forms of "missing the mark" genuine enemies of humankind? Discuss and share. How do these enemies get between humankind and God? Discuss and share.

Jesus goes on to say, in this Ignatian meditation, that whoever wishes to join him in this mission must be willing to labor with him, "so that by following me in suffering, he may follow me in glory." What do you and your study group think Jesus means by saying that disciples must be willing to follow him in suffering? Can you give any examples from the Gospel where Jesus' life led to suffering? Do the values Jesus expresses here complement or contradict the prevailing values of our society? To help you focus this examination, contrast the values that find expression in magazine and television advertising with the values that find expression in Jesus' words and actions. What does it mean to follow Jesus in glory? How are suffering and glory two essential ingredients of what it means to be Jesus' disciple? Discuss and share.

4. I invite you and your study group to reflect on what it means to be a disciple of Jesus. Have each member of your study group list five things that they think are essential elements of being a disciple of Jesus. Discuss and share.

Now I invite you and your study group to consider Jesus' teaching on discipleship as it is found in the Gospel of Mark, 8:22–10:52. Read these texts over as a group. Notice that this section on discipleship begins and ends with the healing of a blind person. How do the disciples demonstrate that they are blind to the true meaning of Christ's teaching in this section? How many times does Jesus predict his passion? According to Jesus' teaching, what place do suffering and dying have in the life of a disciple? What are some of the ways that we soften or turn a "blind eye" to this dimension of discipleship? Discuss and share.

Now I invite you to read and reflect on 1 Corinthians 1:18-31. In what ways is the doctrine of the cross considered foolishness? In what ways is the doctrine of the cross considered a stumbling block? In what ways is the doctrine of the cross considered wisdom?

After you and your study group have concluded this series of reflections and discussions, I invite each member of your group to once again draw up a list of five essential ingredients of what it means to be a disciple of Jesus. Once everyone has drawn up this list, share the lists and discuss them. What differences, if any, do you notice between your initial lists and the most recent ones? If there are any significant changes, what was the catalyst of those changes for people? Discuss and share.

5. Scene One explores things that people fear. We call these phobias. One of the fears mentioned is xenophobia. What are some of the different shapes that xenophobia has taken and is taking in our society today? Do some of the recent propositions passed in California as well as legislation in the United States Congress on "illegal immigration" reflect a certain xenophobic mentality? Why or why not? Explain.

What guidelines do the scriptures give us regarding attitudes and behaviors toward the stranger? Reflect on the following scriptural passages about strangers and discuss their relevance to our attitudes and behavior toward strangers. (1) Exodus 23:9: "You shall not oppress a resident stranger; you know the heart of a stranger, for you were strangers in the land of Egypt." (2) Jeremiah 7:5-7: "For if you truly amend your ways and your doings, if you truly act justly with one another, if you do not oppress the stranger...then I will dwell with you in this place...." (3) Matthew 25:31-46: "...I was a stranger and you welcomed me...And when was it we saw you a stranger and welcomed you?...Truly I tell you, just as you did it to one of the least of these who are members of my family, you did it to me." (4) Hebrews 13:1-2: "Let mutual love continue. Do not neglect to show hospitality to strangers, for by doing that some have entertained angels without knowing it."

St. Benedict, in his *Rule,* instructs the monks: *"Hospes venit. Christus venit."* ("A guest/stranger comes. Christ comes.") Why does St. Benedict encourage the monks to regard and treat strangers the same way they would regard and treat Christ? How do the scriptural and Benedictine attitudes toward strangers compare and contrast with our contemporary attitudes toward strangers, immigrants, and foreigners? Discuss and share.

Have you ever been a stranger in a country where you didn't know the language or the local customs? What difference did it make if/when someone understood your confusion and alienation and somehow made you feel welcome? Discuss and share.

6. The Host, in Scene One, talks about *racism* and *sexism.* What is racism? What are some of racism's obvious and subtle expressions? Discuss and share. What is sexism? What are some of sexism's obvious and subtle expressions? Discuss and share. The Host refers to racism and sexism as diseases. What do you and your study group think the Host means by this? How are racism and sexism diseases? The Host contends that "fear and ignorance" are the roots of these diseases. How

do fear and ignorance find expression in racism and sexism? Discuss and share. The Host goes on to say that "truth" is the antidote to diseases like racism and sexism. Do you and your study group agree or disagree with this analysis? Explain. Why would someone fear the truth, especially if "the truth will set you free"? Discuss and share.

7. Why are the six people in Scene Four wearing chains on their wrists? What do these chains represent? What are some of the different attitudes and behaviors that imprison groups of people? Whom does Person-1 represent? What kind of wisdom might Native Americans have that would enable us to live peacefully with our environment? Discuss and share. Whom do the other people in Scene Four represent? Discuss and share.

How has the history of successive immigrations in the United States been a record of our country's inability to genuinely "welcome the stranger"? Discuss and share. Who are the strangers in our country or state or city or church or school today that we find it difficult to welcome? Discuss strategies for relearning and reclaiming the Christian virtue of hospitality. How is hospitality a primary expression of an incarnational spirituality? In light of this, read, reflect and discuss the following scriptural calls to embody hospitality in our dealings with strangers and friends. (1) Romans 12:13; (2) 1 Timothy 3:2; (3) Titus 1:8; (4) 1 Peter 4:9.

8. "Where there is no vision, the people perish" (Prov 29:18). Get a copy of Dr. Martin Luther King, Jr.'s famous "I Have a Dream" speech. Is this a dream or vision of America that you share? Why or why not? Did the dream/vision die when Dr. King was killed? Why or why not? To what extent has any or all of Dr. King's dream or vision been realized? What keeps us from building or realizing Dr. King's dream/vision? What concrete steps could you and your study group take to help Dr. King's dream/vision become a reality in your school, your church, your state, our country and the world?

7. The Temptations of Jesus

(Matthew 4:1-11)

Then Jesus was led up by the Spirit into the wilderness to be tempted by the devil. And he fasted forty days and forty nights, and afterward he was hungry. And the tempter came and said to him, "If you are the Son of God, command these stones to become loaves of bread." But he answered, "It is written, 'Man shall not live by bread alone, but by every word that proceeds from the mouth of God.'" Then the devil took him to the holy city, and set him on the pinnacle of the temple, and said to him, "If you are the Son of God, throw yourself down; for it is written, 'He will give his angels charge of you,' and 'On their hands they will bear you up, lest you strike your foot against a stone.'" Jesus said to him, "Again it is written, 'You shall not tempt the Lord your God.'" Again, the devil took him to a very high mountain, and showed him all the kingdoms of the world and the glory of them; and he said to him, "All these I will give you, if you will fall down and worship me." Then Jesus said to him, "Begone, Satan! for it is written, 'You shall worship the Lord your God and him only shall you serve.'" Then the devil left him, and behold, angels came and ministered to him.

Lifestyles of a Lenten People

CAST

Host (Laura)	Mayor
Mark	Fr. Ching
Christi	Krista
God-1	Anne
God-2	Keith
God-3	Tarie
Person-1	Kristie
Roommate-1 (Cari)	Roommate-2 (Christi)

SCENE ONE

HOST:

Welcome everyone to the hottest Religious Studies game show in town, "Who Is Your God?" And now, let's have a warm welcome for this week's contestant, Mark Lang. [Mark comes on the stage accompanied by applause.] Welcome, Mark. Tell us a little bit about the God you believe in.

MARK:

[During this entire scene Mark has Christi's hand in his. He does not look at her but gestures with her hand in his, etc.] Well, Laura, it's taken me a long time, but I believe in a God who is with me during the difficult and enjoyable experiences of my life. I believe in a God who is like a very good and trusted friend.

HOST:

Well isn't that precious! I'll tell you what, Mark, you can believe in that God or the God behind Door Number One.

GOD-1:

Does this ring a bell, Mark? "I'm making a list. I'm checking it twice. I know if you've been naughty or nice." Or how about this? "Your conscience hath a thousand several tongues and every tongue cries out: Guilty! Guilty!" You know something, Mark, you're a nice guy. And you know what they say: "Nice guys finish last!" You say you try your best. Try-ers are liars, Mark. Remember this: "The road to hell is paved with good intentions!"

HOST:

What do you say, Mark?

MARK:

Well, Laura. There were times in my life when I believed God was related to Judge Wapner. But the God I believe in has to see more than my faults and my failings. The God I believe in doesn't use threats or fear to move me.

HOST:

Well if the God behind Door Number One was not your cup of tea, perhaps you'll prefer the God behind the Curtain.

GOD-2:

Mark, have I got a deal for you. Let me make it absolutely clear, I will not be undersold! I will match and sweeten any offer you receive from any other God. Now Mark, old buddy, aren't you the guy who told me, when you were just twelve years old, that if I just brought your dog back you'd become a eunuch and go to Mass every day for the rest of your life? You still owe me for that dog. But I'm not one to hold a grudge. Let bygones be bygones. Just tell me what you want, Mark. I know we can make a deal. Sí habla español. Remember, amigo, no down payment, easy credit terms. So come on down right now!

HOST:

What do you think, Mark?

MARK:

I'm not sure I'd buy a used car from that God.

HOST:

Well, Mark, maybe you'll be convinced to trade-in the God you believe in for the God behind Door Number Two.

GOD-3:

That's a my baby. Isn't he cute? He gonna make someone a good husband. But as a son he's not so hot. Mark, what's a matter with you. You no love your Mama? You never write. You never call. Why it take so long for you to come and visit? I give you nothing but life. You give me nothing but grief. What did I ever do to you to deserve this? Go ahead, Mark, break your Mama's heart. Stab me in the back. You know something? Sometimes I even wonder if you really my child.

HOST:

Well, Mark, it's time to decide that all-important question: Who Is Your God? Which one will it be?

MARK:

[Mark throws his hands up in frustration. He is holding Christi's hand.] With these choices, I just don't know. I'm not sure I could believe in any of these Gods. [Mark, Christi and the Host freeze as Person-1 comes up and anoints Mark on the forehead. She traces the sign of the cross on him as she says the following:]

PERSON-1:

May the Lord strengthen you to choose and live the values of the Gospel.

SCENE TWO

MAYOR:

[Hits her gavel three times.] This meeting of the Santa Clara City Council will come to order. I have convened this session of the

143

council to hear arguments for and against City Council Resolution Number 2001 which would provide for the erection of a homeless shelter on the edge of Santa Clara University's Campus. I call upon Jesuit Father Brian Ching to speak first.

FR. CHING:

Madam Mayor, Santa Clara University is founded on strong Judeo-Christian values. We hope to instill concern for the poor and marginated of our world in every student who graduates from our school. But I strongly urge you and the members of the City Council to vote against permitting the building of a homeless shelter on the edge of our campus.

Santa Clara has grown tremendously in the past 25 years. As we look to the future, our projected enrollment demands more classrooms and housing. Building such a shelter would seriously restrict potential expansion for the University.

On a personal note, I would like to add that we take great pride in the beauty of our campus. I think it is attractive to many potential students. I am worried about what the presence of such a shelter will do to people's perception of us. I am genuinely concerned that the shelter, given its clientele, could easily become run-down. I am worried about the environmental impact such a shelter will have on our own property.

MAYOR:

The Chair recognizes Krista Hein.

KRISTA:

I am a senior at Santa Clara University. I am a member of Alpha Phi Sorority and a Santa Clara Community Action Program Coordinator. I can't agree with Fr. Ching's caricature of what the presence of homeless people near our campus will do with our property values or cosmetic appearances.

I have experienced those Judeo-Christian values that Fr. Ching spoke of. They have helped me understand that it is our responsibility to share our knowledge, our understanding, our time, our talents, our food and our neighborhood with those who have no place to call their home.

144

MAYOR:

I now call on Mrs. Anne Ensminger.

ANNE:

Madam Mayor and members of the City Council, my oldest son graduated from Santa Clara last June. I currently have two daughters enrolled at the University. The possibility of a homeless shelter being built near or adjacent to the University makes me very uncomfortable. I worry about my children's safety.

The students here are vulnerable and impressionable. Why would we want to expose them to potential danger and violence and everything else a homeless shelter and itinerant population would attract?

How are we parents or the University going to prepare our sons, our daughters and our students to succeed, "to make it in the real world" with these constant reminders of that element of society that "gave up," that "failed," or "never really tried"?

MAYOR:

We will now hear from Mr. Keith Schwartz, Director of the Julian St. Inn.

KEITH:

I would just like to say that people fear what they do not know. There is a lot of misinformation floating around these chambers this evening, Madam Mayor, about the homeless. I run a shelter and most of the people I deal with are not there because they want to be. Our society has made it difficult or impossible for many of them to lead the simplest of lives.

I have had a long and satisfying relationship with Santa Clara University and her students. I believe that education which calls itself Christian teaches people compassion. It teaches them what "loving your neighbor" means not in the abstract but the concrete. It leads people to understand what brings their brothers and sisters pain. It moves them to work, in some small way, to relieve that pain, to correct that injustice, to heal that wound.

I urge you to allow this shelter to be built.

145

Once Upon a Mystery

MAYOR:

I now call on Doctor Tarie Regan, Dean of the College of Arts and Sciences at SCU.

TARIE:

There was a time and a place for such a measure, for such a shelter. That time has passed. I believe that the construction of such a shelter and its relative proximity to our school would distract students from what we are really about educationally. I do not see how making it easier for people to do service in the community contributes to the attainment of our time-honored educational goals. I strongly urge you to vote against this proposal.

MAYOR:

And finally I call upon Kristie Schindele who is a Santa Clara student currently working with the Eastside Project.

KRISTIE:

I always thought that the scriptures taught us that everyone is equal in God's eyes. Maybe I was wrong. I always thought the Gospels taught Jesus had a special love for the poor, the marginated, the outcasts of society. Maybe I was wrong. I always thought faith was really revealed not in the wonderful words we said but in the simple, loving actions we performed. Maybe I was wrong. I always thought a Christian education would challenge us and teach us how to share, how to be compassionate, how to hunger and thirst and work for justice and equality for all. Maybe I was wrong. I thought Santa Clara University prided itself in educating "men and women for others." Maybe I was wrong.

MAYOR:

We will now vote on City Council Resolution Number 2001. All those in favor of allowing a homeless shelter to be built on the border of Santa Clara University, please indicate by raising your right hand. [All freeze. Person-1 goes and anoints the foreheads of the seven members of this scene and then says the following:]

PERSON-1:

> May the Lord strengthen you to choose and live the values of the Gospel.

SCENE THREE

R-MATE-1:

> [During this scene Roommate-1 is involved in continual activity. She is a driven person. She is a bundle of energy seeking expression. She begins by doing some basic calisthenics.]

R-MATE-2:

> [Walks onto the stage and sits down.] Hi, Cari.

R-MATE-1:

> Hi, Christi. Where have you been?

R-MATE-2:

> I just came from Mass.

R-MATE-1:

> You're not becoming a "religious fanatic" on me, are you?

R-MATE-2:

> No, I just remembered it was Ash Wednesday and thought I'd wander over to the Mission and see what was going on.

R-MATE-1:

> Oh my God, I completely forgot.

R-MATE-2:

> Not to worry, there are two more Masses at 7 and 10 p.m.

R-MATE-1:

> I'd love to go, Christi, but I can't afford the time. Crew season is upon us and I'm in woefully bad shape. Mind if I borrow a few of your ashes? [Roommate-1 takes some of the ashes on Roommate-2's forehead and traces them on her own forehead.]

R-MATE-2:

> I don't mind, Cari, but it's not the ashes that are important. It's what they represent.

R-MATE-1:

> What do you mean?

R-MATE-2:

> Well, I think they represent our call and commitment to change in our life where we need to change. Have you thought about what you're going to do during Lent?

R-MATE-1:

> I'm going to give up my insulin.

R-MATE-2:

> Don't be silly, Cari. If you gave up your insulin you'd die.

R-MATE-1:

> Well, then, I'm going to give up green beans.

R-MATE-2:

> You don't eat vegetables, Cari. You've already given them up. Besides, I don't think Lent is about giving things up.

R-MATE-1:

> So what are you going to do?

R-MATE-2:

> I'm not sure. Sometimes I feel like a hamster on a spinning wheel what with the pace of the quarter system. I'm always struggling to keep my head above water. I think this Lent I'd like to take some time out. I'd like to stop, step back and take a long look at the direction of my life.

R-MATE-1:

> Well that should take about ten minutes. Sounds like a short Lent to me!

R-MATE-2:

> Cari, I'm serious. This Lent I want to pay attention to what I really value.

R-MATE-**1**:

> I'll tell you what I'd really value right now: Spring Break!

R-MATE-**2**:

> I want to listen to the stories that the actions of my life tell about what is really important to me. And I want to see if those values are the same as the values of the Gospel I keep saying I believe in.

R-MATE-**1**:

> And if they're not?

R-MATE-**2**:

> Then I think I'll have the first clue about the type of conversion I'm being called to, about what I need to change in my life.

R-MATE-**1**:

> Whewie! What's gotten into you, woman?

R-MATE-**2**:

> I'm not sure I completely understand myself, Cari. A number of things have come together, for some reason, and really hit me at this time. Watching you exercise all year for Crew's short season reminds me that times of preparation are important. I hope that whatever we choose to do in Lent will prepare us to truly be Easter People. [Roommate-1 and Roommate-2 freeze. Person-1 comes up and anoints each of them and says the following words:]

PERSON-**1**:

> May the Lord strengthen you to choose and live the values of the Gospel.

—FINIS—

PROPS

1. One (1) Gavel to be used by the Mayor in Scene Two.
2. One (1) Bar Stool or Table that the Mayor uses to hit his gavel.
3. One (1) Podium for the different speakers in Scene Two.
4. Ashes in the form of a cross on the forehead of Roommate-2 in Scene Three.

PRODUCTION NOTES

This biblical drama was designed and performed as part of a liturgy on the first Sunday of Lent, Cycle "A." The Biblical Explorers attempted to wrestle with the meaning of "the temptations of Christ" in our lives today. The presence of Person-1 anointing characters with the sign of the cross in each scene and saying: "May the Lord strengthen you to choose and live the values of the Gospel" was a conscious attempt to build on the words and actions associated with the beginning of Lent. Four days earlier, on Ash Wednesday, ashes were blessed and distributed with the words: "Turn away from sin and be faithful to the Gospel."

Lent is a time in the liturgical year when Christians prepare in a special way for the celebration of Easter. Lent has been described as "The Church on retreat." The three scenes in this biblical drama invite you and your study group to examine three aspects of your faith life during these forty days of Lenten observance: (1) your images of God, (2) your response to the voiceless and powerless in the community, and (3) what shape the traditional practices of Lent (praying, fasting and almsgiving) will take in your observance of Lent.

There are specific references to Santa Clara University. These are places where you will have to adapt the dramas to your own locations and needs. The issues that the Santa Clara students deal with in these three scenes have much more than local or provincial significance. Lent can be a time of retreat when you and your faith community can examine your images of God and how they are operative in both the life and the worship of your community. Lent can be a time to reflect on your faith community's response to the voiceless and powerless around you. Lent can be a time for your faith community to consider what they do, symbolized perhaps by the traditional corporal works of mercy, that helps "the least of our brothers and sisters" to experience the liberating power of the Gospel in their everyday life. It can also be a time for your faith community to consider what they stop doing, symbolized perhaps by the biblical imagery of blindness, deafness, muteness and paralysis, that prevents "the least of our brothers and sisters" from experiencing the liberating power of the Gospel in their everyday life.

REFLECTION QUESTIONS AND EXERCISES

1. John L. McKenzie, S.J., in his commentary on the Gospel of Matthew, suggests that the temptations and Jesus' response to them define the true character of his mission. McKenzie concludes that "the temptation comes not to Jesus but to the Church which carries on his mission" *(Jerome Biblical Commentary)*.

I invite you and your study group to read and reflect on the beginning of Jesus' public ministry as it is described in Luke 4:14-21. According to this passage of the Gospel, what comprises the mission of Jesus? In other words, what does Jesus believe he was sent to do? Discuss and share. What does it mean to "bring good news to the poor"? What shapes might this good news take? What does it mean "to proclaim release to the captives and recovery of sight to the blind"? Who are the captives? Who are the blind? What does it mean "to let the oppressed go free"? Who are the oppressed? What would constitute freedom for them? What does it mean "to proclaim the year of the Lord's favor"? Discuss and share.

Since we consider ourselves disciples and followers of Christ, how does his mission shape our own? Who are "the poor" in our world today? What good news are we called to bring them? How do we do this? Who are the captives in our world today? What in our society and world binds them? What would release mean for them? Who are the blind in our society today? What are they incapable of seeing? How might they recover their sight? Who are the oppressed in our culture and society today? What shapes might release take for them? What would a "year of the Lord's favor" mean for our society and world today? Discuss and share.

How is the story of the three temptations of Jesus critical in our own life and ministry? Remember that the Chinese use two characters for the word "crisis." One character means "danger" and the other character means "opportunity." How does the story of the temptations of Jesus in the desert remind us of the "danger" and difficulty of following Christ today? Discuss and share. How does the story of the temptations of Jesus in the desert remind us of the "opportunity" and hope of following Christ today? Discuss and share.

2. Brother Norbert and the Monks of the Weston Priory have written a song entitled "Come Back To Me." Lent is a time of reconciliation and

151

forgiveness. Lent offers Christians the invitation and opportunity to come back to the Lord with all their heart. I invite you and your study group to consider some of your images of God. You may wish to think of some attribute or quality or characteristic of God like "Compassionate God," "Gentle God," "Good and gracious God," "Faithful and loving God," that can be used in a Lenten litany.

After you and your study group have brainstormed on these different images and descriptions of how we can experience God, I invite you to do a simple prayer exercise in which one member of your group proclaims the image of God and invites the group response of: "Return to you with all our heart." It could be additionally effective to begin this litany prayer and end it with the singing of a few verses of the song "Come Back to Me."

Let me give you an example of how the litany might go. Remember: don't be limited by these suggestions. Allow your group to explore the richness and variety of ways that God can be experienced, described and imagined.

Person: Gentle God, help us…
Group: Return to you with all our heart.
Person: Compassionate God, help us…
Group: Return to you with all our heart.
Person: Faithful and loving God, help us…
Group: Return to you with all our heart.
Person: You are light for our journey. Help us…
Group: Return to you with all our heart.
Person: You are the Word that satisfies our hunger. Help us…
Group: Return to you with all our heart.
Person: You are strength for our weary limbs. Help us…
Group: Return to you with all our heart.
Person: You are the Good Shepherd who seeks us out and finds us when we are lost. Help us…
Group: Return to you with all our heart.
Person: You are the prodigal parent who waits for us with longing and love to come home. Help us…
Group: Return to you with all our heart.
Person: You are the least of our brothers and sisters. Help us…
Group: Return to you with all our heart.
Person: You are the Way. Help us…

Group: Return to you with all our heart.
Person: You are the Truth. Help us…
Group: Return to you with all our heart.
Person: You are Life. Help us…
Group: Return to you with all our heart.

3. In Scene One, why is Mark holding Christi's hand throughout the entire scene? Who does Christi represent? What are some of the masculine qualities or characteristics or images of God in the Bible? How do people experience, describe and image God in the Old Testament and in the New Testament? How has the Church experienced, described and imaged God in the Christian Tradition? Here you might draw upon the writings of St. Columbanus, St. Teresa of Avila, St. Francis of Assisi, St. Ignatius of Loyola, Meister Eckhart, Julian of Norwich, Archbishop Romero, Thomas Merton, Dorothy Day and others. Which of these experiences, descriptions and images appeal to you? Discuss and share.

What are some of the feminine qualities or characteristics or images of God in the Bible? How do people experience, describe and image God with feminine qualities or characteristics in the Old Testament and the New Testament? How has the Church experienced, described and imaged God with feminine qualities or characteristics in the Christian Tradition? Discuss and share.

What words would you and your study group use to describe God-1 in Scene One? Discuss and share. What words would you and your study group use to describe God-2? Discuss and share. What words would you and your study group use to describe God-3? Discuss and share. What words would you and your study group use to describe God at this time in your life? Discuss and share.

4. Scene One invites each of you to reflect and share who the God is that you experience and worship in life. Leo Rock, a Jesuit spiritual director and clinical psychologist, once said that Christians meet God the way they meet other people in life. He described four types of meetings. First, there is the *casual meeting* in which two people on opposite sidewalks pass each other at some distance. Second, there is the *mediated meeting* in which one person is introduced to another person by a third person who knows both of the other people. Third, there is the *business meeting* in which the purpose of the meeting is an agenda. When the agenda is finished, so is the meeting. Fourth, there is the *intimate meeting* when two

friends bask in the presence of each other. What they say or what they do is much less important than the fact that they are lovingly in each other's presence.

Scene One asks the question "Who is your God?" A further question, based on Leo Rock's four types of human meetings, might be "How do you meet God in your life?" When you experience God is it a *casual meeting?* Do you meet and keep God at a comfortable distance? When you experience God is it a *mediated meeting?* Does something like scripture or religious art or spiritual reading or even ritual action facilitate your meeting with God? Are you trusting and relying on someone else's experience and description of God? When you experience God is it a *business meeting?* Do you have an agenda you want to go over with God? Once you have spoken your piece, is the meeting over? Is there ever room in this type of meeting to listen to what God might say in response to your agenda? When you experience God is it an *intimate meeting?* Do you ever experience God as friend? Do you ever simply come together with God and spend time in one another's presence? Discuss and share.

5. In Scene Two, Fr. Ching voices his concern about locating a homeless shelter near his university campus. He says: "I am worried about what the presence of such a shelter will do to people's perception of us." What do you and your study group think he means by this? Which characters in this scene do you and your study group think articulate Gospel values? Discuss and share.

What evidence do we have in the Gospels about the people who comprised Jesus' ministry? Discuss and share. I invite you and your study group to read and reflect on Luke 7:31-35 and then discuss the following questions. With whom did Jesus spend time in his life and ministry? What opinion did some people have of Jesus because he ate and drank with sinners? What opinion did some people have of Jesus because he told stories to prostitutes and sinners and listened to the stories they had to tell him? Did people's perception of Jesus determine his life and ministry? Did people's opinion of Jesus determine what he said or what he did in his life and ministry? If so, why? If not, what did determine what Jesus said and did in his life and ministry? Discuss and share. You and your study group might also find it helpful to explore the meals of Jesus that are recorded in any one of the Gospels. Eugene La Verdiere has an excellent book entitled *Dining in the Kingdom*

(Chicago: Liturgy Training Publications, 1994) which examines the meal accounts that are found in Luke's Gospel and the clues they give us about the meaning of the Eucharist in our life and ministry today. How are Jesus' life and ministry, his attitudes and behaviors, a model and challenge for our life and ministry today? Discuss and share.

6. In Scene Three, Roommate-2 describes Lent as a time "to pay attention to what I really value." How can Lent be a time to pay attention to what I really value? What are some of the values of the Gospel? You will discover many of the Gospel values in the words and actions of Jesus.

How are Gospel values counter-cultural? How do the values of the Gospel sometimes conflict with the values of a consumer society like the United States of America? What are some practical ways we can give Gospel values expression in our relationships with those who are voiceless and powerless in our society today? John Kavanaugh's book *Following Christ in a Consumer Society* (Maryknoll, New York: Orbis Books, 1981) continues to be a challenging and thought-provoking commentary on how possible it is to live a Christian life in our society. (See also Bruce C. Birch and Larry L. Rasmussen, *The Predicament of the Prosperous.* Philadelphia: The Westminster Press, 1978.)

7. Roommate-2 suggests that Lent is a time "to listen to the stories that the actions of my life tell about what is really important to me. And I want to see if those values are the same as the values of the Gospel I keep saying I believe in." What stories do the actions of your life tell about what is really important to you? Discuss and share.

To what types of change or conversion might each member of your study group be called this Lent? Discuss and share. What is one attitude that you and your study group would like to change this Lent? How could you go about changing it? What is one concrete step that you and your study group can take together to change this attitude so that it is more reflective of Gospel values? Discuss and share.

What is one behavior that you and your study group would like to change this Lent? How could you go about changing it? What is one concrete step that you and your study group can take to change this behavior so that it is more reflective of Gospel values? Discuss and share.

8. Throughout this biblical drama, Person-1 prays: "May the Lord strengthen you to choose and live the values of the Gospel." In Celtic

spirituality, there is a tremendous sense of the presence and protection of the Trinity in each Christian's life. Consider the different persons of the Trinity. How does the first person of the Trinity, God the Creator, strengthen you to choose and live the values of the Gospel? Discuss and share. How does the second person of the Trinity, God the Redeemer, strengthen you to choose and live the values of the Gospel? Discuss and share. How does the third person of the Trinity, God the Holy Spirit, strengthen you to choose and live the values of the Gospel? Discuss and share.

How does God strengthen us to choose and live the values of the Gospel through liturgical celebrations? How does the liturgy of the Word strengthen us to choose and live the values of the Gospel? How does sharing the Eucharist strengthen us to choose and live the values of the Gospel? Discuss and share?

How do the lives of the saints strengthen us to choose and live the values of the Gospel? Discuss and share. Here it would be good to select one or two saints to examine and discuss.

How do the corporal works of mercy strengthen us to choose and live the values of the Gospel? Discuss and share.

8. Jesus Blesses the Children

(Mark 10:13-16)

And they were bringing children to him, that he might touch them; and the disciples rebuked them. But when Jesus saw it he was indignant, and said to them, "Let the children come to me, do not hinder them; for to such belongs the kingdom of God. Truly, I say to you, whoever does not receive the kingdom of God like a child shall not enter it." And he took them in his arms and blessed them, laying his hands upon them.

Teach Me Your Ways, O Lord

CAST

Director
Have-1 (Michele)
Have-2 (Ron)
Have-3 (Rosemary)
Have-Not (Cari)
Hostess-1
Hostess-2
Hostess-3
Audience
Student-1 (Molly)
Student-2 (Alison)

Host-1 (Mark)
Host-2 (Sally)
Mr. Konk
Mrs. Dole
Homeless-1 (Brian)
Homeless-2 (Tarie)
Homeless-3 (Krista)
Homeless-4 (Dan)
Homeless-5 (Kristie)
Homeless-6

SCENE ONE

HOST-1:

Please welcome the "Haves." [Applause] And also welcome the "Have-Nots." [Applause] They're going to have it out tonight on this special edition of "Family Feud." [Applause. Both families come down to their contestant positions.]

And a big Family Feud welcome to the Haves. [Applause] Michele, you're the Captain of your team. Introduce the other members of your family to us.

HAVE-1:

Well, Mark, this is my husband Ron.

HOST-1:

Welcome, Ron.

HAVE-1:

And my *older* sister Rosemary.

HAVE-3:

Only by six months!

HOST-1:

Welcome to all of you Haves! [Pause] And now let's meet the Have-Not Family. Cari, welcome to you and...where are the rest of your family?

HAVE-NOT:

I don't have a family, Mark.

HOST-1:

Oh, I see. Well, let's not cry over spilt milk. Come on, contestants, let's get down to business. Michele and Cari, we surveyed our studio audience here this evening, and their top four answers are up on our board. Get your hands on your buzzers. Here's what we asked them: What do you consider are the necessities of life? [Michele and Cari go for their buzzers but Cari hits hers first. Throughout this scene the other members of the cast make sound effects for the right answer, wrong answer, clarification and applause.] Cari, what do you say?

HAVE-NOT:

Food.

HOST-1:

Show us "Food"! [The supporting cast make the sound for a wrong answer and Hostess-1 holds up a red "X".] Michele, what do you say?

HAVE-1:

Microwave.

HOST-1:

Show us "Microwave"! [The supporting cast make the sound for the right answer and the panel on the board for answer No. 4 is turned over revealing the word "Microwave."] O.K., Michele, you and the Haves control the board. What do you want to do? Will you play or pass? [The Haves shout out their views.]

HAVE-1:

We'll pass, Mark.

HOST-1:

O.K., Cari, here's a chance for the Have-Nots to steal the game. We've got three more answers from our studio audience up there. Give me one of their answers to the question: What do you consider are the necessities of life?

HAVE-NOT:

Well I'd say "Shelter."

HOST-1:

Show us "Shelter"! [The supporting cast makes the sound for the wrong answer and Hostess-2 holds up a red "X".] Sorry, Cari, that's not up there. Try again.

HAVE-NOT:

I'd say "Clothing." That's a necessity of life.

HOST-1:

If "Clothing" is up there, the Have-Nots are halfway there. Show us "Clothing"! [The supporting cast makes the sound for the wrong answer while Hostess-1 joins Hostess-2 in holding up a red "X".] I'm sorry, darlin', that wasn't one of the answers this audience came up with. But you've still got one more chance. What else do you think they would have said was "a necessity of life"?

HAVE-NOT:

I'd say a "Job."

HOST-1:

If "Job" is up there, you're still alive. If not, you may want to consider Hari Cari, because the Haves will get a chance to win the game. Let's see if you got it. Show us "Job"! [The supporting cast makes the sound for a wrong answer and Hostess-1 holds up a red "X" while Hostess-2 holds up two red "Xs".] O.K., Haves, this is your chance to win the game. Give us one of the answers that the studio audience here gave us to the question: What do you consider are the necessities of life? Now, Michele, you can get help from the other members of your family and then decide.

HAVE-**3**:

What about a "summer home"?

HAVE-**2**:

I'd say a "BMW" or some "nice car."

HAVE-**1**:

I like "credit card."

HOST-**1**:

O.K., Michele, moment of decision. Which answer will it be?

HAVE-**1**:

We'll go with "credit card."

HOST-**1**:

All right, darlin', if it's there, you win the game. Show us "credit card"! [A beeping sound occurs.] Michele, you're on the right track, but our judges want you to be more specific.

HAVE-**3**:

Citicorp Mastercard?

HAVE-**2**:

Visa Platinum?

HAVE-**1**:

How about "American Express Gold Card"?

HOST-**1**:

Show us "American Express Gold Card"! [The sound goes off indicating a right answer and panel No. 3 of the game board is turned over by Hostess-1 and Hostess-2. There is thunderous applause.] Now let's see what those other two answers by our studio audience were. The No. 1 answer was…. [Hostess-1 and Hostess-2 turn over panel No. 1] "A Nice Car". And the No. 2 answer was…. [Hostess-1 and Hostess-2 turn over panel No. 2.] "Summer Home." Cari, I'm afraid we're going to have to say goodbye to you. But we've got some nice departing gifts for you, including the new video home version of "Family Feud."

HAVE-NOT:

But I don't have a television or a VCR.

HOST-1:

Oh well, Cari, when you do have them you will really enjoy this prize. [Pause] All right, Haves, are you ready to play for the big money? [Haves nod "yes"!] Well, we'll get right to that after these important commercial announcements. [All the characters freeze. The Choir leads the congregation in singing the antiphon "Teach Me Your Ways, O Lord." As they finish with the antiphon, the players from Scene One move out of the acting area and the players in Scene Two move into position.]

SCENE TWO

DIRECTOR:

[All of the players are seated in a semi-circle. Host-2 is standing in front of them with a microphone. The Director starts giving hand signals and counting out loud.] Five, four, three, two, one, and you're rolling! [Director points to Host-2.]

HOST-2:

Welcome back to the Sally Jessy-Raphael Show. Our subject today is: "Homelessness: Fact or Fiction." We have with us Mr. Peter Miron-Konk who is Director of the San Jose Urban Ministries. Welcome, Mr. Konk.

KONK:

Thank you, Sally. It's good to be here.

HOST-2:

From Washington, D.C., we are pleased to have with us the

Secretary of Health, Education & Welfare, Mrs. Elizabeth "Not-On-The" Dole.

DOLE:

I'm always happy to help dismiss some of the misinformation circulating about homelessness in this great country of ours.

HOST-2:

And we are particularly happy to have three people with us who have experienced first-hand what homelessness is all about. Tarie, would you tell us how long you have been homeless?

HOMELESS-2:

My husband and I, together with our three children, were homeless for two years. We recently moved into permanent housing. It's taken us a long time but we're slowly getting back on our feet, Sally.

HOST-2:

And Brian, how long have you been homeless?

HOMELESS-1:

Four months, Sally.

HOST-2:

And Krista, how long have you been homeless?

HOMELESS-3:

For most of my life, Sally.

HOST-2:

Well let's get a question from one of our viewers who has phoned in. Go ahead, caller.

AUDIENCE-1:

Yeah. I have just one question. Why don't these lazy bums quit whining and moaning? Why don't they get off their collective "duffs" and get a job?

HOST-2:

Panel, how would you respond to our caller?

DOLE:

> I would tend to agree with our caller. As our former President once said: "If people are homeless, it's because they want to be."

HOMELESS-2:

> My husband was making a six figure salary. We didn't choose homelessness. We were plunged into it by circumstances beyond our control.

HOMELESS-1:

> It's tough to get a job when you don't have a permanent address. When I go looking for work, I don't even have clean clothes for an interview. A lot of people never get past appearances. And when I don't have clothes, let alone clean clothes, to wear, what am I supposed to do?

HOMELESS-3:

> I want to work but I have to travel everywhere by bus. It takes so long to get across town by bus. And I didn't get much education growing up. So I have a hard time understanding and filling out all the forms they give me.

KONK:

> The most common misconception of the homeless is that they are lazy. The second most common misconception about the homeless is that the majority of them are alcoholics or drug addicts— the dregs of society. The fact is that the largest number of homeless in America are single mothers and children. Try telling a hungry three-year-old that the reason why he's so poor and homeless is because he's just too lazy to go out and get a job. Try telling that single mother with three small children that she should leave her children on the street and go get a job.

HOST-2:

> I think a question that's on everyone's mind, and I want to ask this as delicately as I can, is: "What is it like to be homeless?"

HOMELESS-1:

> You lose your self-respect very quickly. You become depressed.

You want to numb the pain, so sometimes you do turn to alcohol or drugs. It helps you forget for a little while.

HOMELESS-3:

It's like being at the bottom of a hole. You're looking up at the opening but you can't figure how in the world to get out.

HOMELESS-2:

You change very quickly. When you don't even have a place to stay, your attitudes about shelters and the homeless change dramatically. And even though we have a home of our own again, the children and I find that haunting question lurking in the back of our minds: "Will it happen again?"

HOST-2:

So what words would each of you on the panel have for us who are watching this show?

DOLE:

In the words of our former First Lady, "Just Say No to Homelessness."

HOMELESS-3:

What I need most is a chance! There have to be places available that can give us enough care and support to go on.

HOMELESS-1:

There need to be more opportunities to get off the streets. We need education. We need to learn skills that will help us find jobs.

HOMELESS-2:

When I was homeless what I needed most was emotional help and some compassion.

KONK:

I think what we have to realize is that the homeless in our society are like children. They are on the bottom rung of society. They are without status or power or value or voice. We have to find ways not only to educate the homeless but to educate our society about the ways we promote and perpetuate homelessness. We need to become a power for these powerless and a voice for these voiceless.

HOST-2:

I want to thank all of our guests for being with us today. I'm sorry that our time is up. Be sure and tune in tomorrow when we will take a hard look at: "The Holocaust: Fact or Fiction." [Director holds up "Applause" card.]

DIRECTOR:

And cut. That's it, everybody. Please clear the set. We have to get things ready for the filming of "Silver Spoons." [Dole, Konk and Host-2 exchange greetings as Dole and Konk leave the acting area in different directions. Director comes up to the three homeless people.] I'm sorry, you'll have to go home now.

HOMELESS-2:

We haven't got a home.

DIRECTOR:

Yes, well...you have to get out of here because we need to set this stage set up for another show. [Director goes off doing busy work. Homeless-1 goes to Host-2.]

HOMELESS-1:

Excuse us, Mrs. Raphael. We were told we would be paid $250 for appearing on your show. That's the reason we did it. We need the money. Right now none of us can even afford to stay in a shelter. We borrowed money to take the bus down here to the studio. Even if you can't give us our check, if you could just give us $66 of it we could stay in the Shelter for three weeks.

HOST-2:

[Goes to the Director] They were promised they'd get their money before they had to leave. They need it, Jenny. What should I do?

DIRECTOR:

The checks aren't ready yet. You know that takes time. Why don't you get a phone number or a mailing address. We'll contact them as soon as those checks are ready.

HOMELESS-3:

Excuse me, ma'am, but I couldn't help but overhear you. The problem is that we don't have a phone. And to have an address you need a home. We don't have either.

DIRECTOR:

Well, I'm very sorry about the inconvenience but there just isn't anything I can do. Check back with us in a few days and we should have your checks.

HOMELESS-1:

But...

HOMELESS-2:

But...

DIRECTOR:

No more "Buts." CLEAR THE SET! Start bringing in the props and scenery for "Silver Spoons." [Everyone freezes. The Homeless look at the Congregation puzzled and sad. The Choir leads the Congregation in singing the Antiphon "Teach Me Your Ways, O Lord." The lights begin to dim on the acting area. When the lights are low the actors go to their places in the Congregation and are replaced by the actors for Scene Three.]

SCENE THREE

STUDENT-1:

[Student-1 and Student-2 come into the center acting area.] Alison, where are you off to in such a hurry?

STUDENT-2:

I'm one of the coordinators for the 10 P.M. liturgy in the Mission. I'm supposed to write a petition about the homeless and I haven't got the foggiest idea who the homeless are or what I'm supposed to ask God to give them. How am I supposed to know what they need?

STUDENT-1:

Just include the words "peace" and "happiness" and that ought to satisfy the homeless and God.

STUDENT-2:

> Thanks for the help. Are you going to be there at 10 P.M. to hear my prayerful and artistic triumph?

STUDENT-1:

> I wish I could be there. Unfortunately, I've got to work at the Montgomery Shelter all evening.

STUDENT-2:

> I didn't know you were doing some volunteer work.

STUDENT-1:

> I'm not. Well, I guess I am, but reluctantly. I'm taking that Biblical Drama Class and everyone has to work with the homeless for eight two-hour sessions. I really don't understand why we have to do it. I can't see that it's helping them or me.

STUDENT-2:

> Got to go, Molly. Good luck at the shelter.

STUDENT-1:

> Yeah. And good luck to you on creating that prayer. [Student-1 goes downstage left. Student-2 goes to the lectern upstage right. Student-1 mimes giving out food to three Homeless people who go past her. Student-2 prays the prayer she has made up. She pauses intermittently to allow the Homeless people to speak.]

STUDENT-2:

> Let us pray for the homeless throughout the world.

HOMELESS-4:

> Please, Miss, I know people act as if I'm faceless and nameless, but I've got a name. My name is Dan. Please remember my name when you pray for me. [Dan takes his imaginary tray of food and goes to his seat.]

STUDENT-2:

> That they might experience the peace and happiness of a home...

HOMELESS-5:

> My name is Kristie. My home is a box. At night I live in that box

on a street in your city. [Homeless-5 takes her imaginary tray and sits in one of the chairs next to Homeless-4.]

STUDENT-2:

…and that God might give all the homeless a comfortable life…

HOMELESS-6:

I don't want a comfortable life. I just want a human life. [Homeless-6 takes her imaginary tray and sits in a chair next to Homeless-5.]

STUDENT-2:

And, finally, that God help us see in the homeless our brothers and sisters, and show us ways to reach out to them in their need.

HOMELESS-4:

[Homeless-4 stands.] You can't catch homelessness…[Homeless-4 is then joined by Homeless-5 and Homeless-6 who stand on the next line] but you can help the homeless.

HOMELESS-5:

…but you can help the homeless.

HOMELESS-6:

…but you can help the homeless.

HOMELESS-5:

Please…

HOMELESS-4:

…won't you…

HOMELESS-6:

…help us?

STUDENT-2:

For this, we pray to the Lord. [All the actors freeze as the Choir leads the Congregation in singing the antiphon "Teach Me Your Ways, O Lord." The lights are brought down gradually. When they are down, the players go to their places in the congregation.]

—FINIS—

PROPS

1. Four (4) Bar Stools which the contestants can stand behind during the game show in Scene One.
2. One (1) Game Show Board on which the correct answers are hidden. Those answers are: (1) A Nice Car; (2) Summer Home; (3) American Express Gold Card; (4) Microwave. These answers are covered by pieces of paper and only revealed at the appropriate time. The board must be big enough for the congregation to see.
3. Three (3) Poster Board Cards with a red "X" on them.
4. One (1) Poster Board Card with the word "Applause" printed on it in large letters.

PRODUCTION NOTES

During my eleven years at Santa Clara University, the President's Office would regularly sponsor an Institute that invited the examination of some current issue or event. Departments within the University as well as local and national people who could bring a perspective and expertise not necessarily found in the University were invited to participate. This biblical drama was part of one such Institute entitled "Voice for the Voiceless" which focused on a number of groups of people in our society who have been systematically marginalized. The "homeless" were one such group.

The Institute was held over a period of six months. During that time homelessness was examined from a variety of perspectives including that of homeless people themselves. A special liturgy was celebrated as part of this Institute. The scripture readings chosen were Isaiah 58:1-14 and Mark 10:13-16. The readings spoke about what was acceptable "fasting" or worship to God. The Gospel, with its central image of children, offered an excellent example of the powerless and voiceless in our society today.

There are three vignettes that comprise this biblical drama. The first vignette focuses on a game show. Clearly the homeless person expresses what people need to survive in the world. She speaks of such things as food, shelter, clothing and work. But these are not the "necessities of life" as considered by the studio audience who all come from the first world. This is intended not only as irony but as a comment on the social environment typical of some students who attend private schools. Santa

Clara University ranks as a prestigious private, Catholic, Jesuit university. It is my hope that the congregations and audiences who experience this will not only be amused but shocked by the absurdity of what the studio audience consider the first world necessities of life.

The second vignette was inspired by an actual evening forum of the Institute that involved five homeless men and women from the surrounding cities of Santa Clara and San Jose, California. These men and women bravely shared their stories about the horrific experience of being homeless. All of them had been told that they would receive a speaker's stipend for their participation. At the end of the evening, to everyone's embarrassment, the organizers of the program discovered that they had failed to request and get the stipends for these men and women. One homeless man actually needed the financial assistance to get back to his shelter. Additionally, all those involved in this incident were forced to realize the dilemma of the homeless person who has no bank account and could not cash a stipend that came in the form of a check because he/she has no permanent address and therefore can not set up a bank account.

The third vignette comes out of my experience of teaching liturgy at Santa Clara University for ten years. While I was successful in teaching students that the general pattern of the Prayers of the Faithful or General Intercessions was for the Church, the world, the needy and the local community, I was not able to motivate most students to do anything but pray for the poor, hungry, homeless or victims of violence in the vaguest and most general ways. When students composed prayers that said: "That the homeless may not lose hope" or "That the homeless may experience God's care and protection," I would ask the students: "What will keep the homeless from losing hope?" "Whose attitudes and behaviors will communicate God's care and protection to homeless people?" In this way, I tried to help students realize that we ultimately have to pray that God will transform our hearts so that we will see the homeless and respond to them as God would: compassionately and concretely.

The song "Teach Me Your Ways, O Lord" by Michael B. Lynch served to connect the vignettes together. It also became a powerful meditation on the scriptures and the dramatized homily. The words of the song expressed the spirit of the University Institute. The song became the prayer of all those who gathered for the different Institute presentations that through our examination of the plight of the marginated we might discover how to become a voice for the voiceless and power for the powerless.

While this biblical drama has a cast of eighteen, I frequently had students play more than one role. Always adapt these biblical dramas to your own teaching and worship needs. If you are working with a larger number of people, you have plenty or dramatic roles to distribute. If you are working with a smaller group, utilize the option of people playing more than one character in the drama. Equally important is the need to invite suggestions from the people who are doing this drama with you. Incorporate their dramatic suggestions and adaptations into your performance. This is an essential way that you and your study group make these biblical dramas your own and put your own unique stamp upon them.

REFLECTION QUESTIONS AND EXERCISES

1. According to Isaiah 58:1-14, what is the fast that God chooses? What do you and your study group think it means to "to loose the bonds of injustice"? How do you go about doing this? What is a yoke? Why does God ask for every yoke to be broken? What do you and your study group think it means "to let the oppressed go free"? In what ways are the homeless in our society oppressed? Who or what oppresses them? What are the ways that you and your study group participate consciously or unconsciously in the oppression of the homeless or the freeing of them? Discuss and share.

2. What do you and your study group think it means "to share your bread with the hungry"? How can you do this literally and figuratively? What does it mean "to bring the homeless poor into your home"? What are some of the ways you can do this? When do you and your study group think you see people naked? What might this image mean literally and figuratively? What are some of the ways you can help cover people's nakedness or minister to them in their vulnerability? What do you and your study group think are some of the ways that you "hide yourself from your own kin"? What might be some of the ways you can reveal yourself to them?

The scriptures indicate that when we practice these concrete acts of human kindness or Christian corporal works of mercy, "light," "healing," and "vindication" will result. What do you and your study group think these images of light, healing and vindication mean? How do merciful attitudes and behaviors have the characteristics and qualities of light, healing and vindication? Discuss and share. Why do the scriptures suggest that if you do these things God will answer you when you call and be present to you when you cry for help? Discuss and share.

3. In the Roman Catholic celebration of the Eucharist there is a penitential rite during the Introductory Rites. The communal recitation of the *Confiteor* is the first option. The faith community acknowledges their sins and asks God's forgiveness. In this penitential prayer, each member of the worshiping community says: "I have sinned [that is, missed the mark] through my own fault, in my thoughts and in my words, in what I have done, and what I have failed to do." How have you and your study group "missed the mark" with the poor, the hungry and the homeless in the ways that you have thought about them? Discuss and share. How have you "missed the mark" with the poor, the hungry and the homeless in the ways that you have spoken about them? Discuss and share. How have you and your study group "missed the mark" with the poor, the hungry and the homeless through your attitudes and actions? Discuss and share. How have you "missed the mark" with the poor, the hungry and the homeless by what you have failed to do? Discuss and share.

What do you and your study group think are some practical and concrete steps that you can take to change the ways you think, speak about or act toward the poor, the hungry and the homeless who are part of your community? Discuss and share.

4. In Scene One, what does the *Have Family* consider the necessities of life? What does the *Have-Not Family* consider the necessities of life? What do you and your study group consider as necessities to live a human life? Discuss and share. Are there luxuries in our first world lives that we become dependent on to the point of experiencing them as necessities? Consider the following questions. How long has it been since you have watched television? What is the longest period of time you have not watched television? How long has it been since you have been to the movies? How often do you have the radio or stereo on when you are at home or in the car? What's the longest period of time you have gone without listening to your Walkman, radio or stereo? When is the last time you walked anywhere you had to go over a mile? When is

the last time you took public transportation to your destination? Compare your first world responses with how people in the third world might respond to these same questions. Discuss and share.

In Scene One, Cari is given a video version of *Family Feud* as a consolation prize. She mentions that she doesn't have a television or a VCR. Have you or your study group ever spent time in a place that did not have electricity or modern conveniences? How do you think you would react to such a challenging environment? Keep in mind that people of the third world and groups of people like the poor, the hungry and the homeless in the United States experience such "lack of conveniences" to be a way of life. Discuss and share your reactions to these situations.

What words would you and your study group use to describe Peter Miron-Konk's understanding of homelessness in Scene Two? Discuss and share. What words would you and your study group use to describe Elizabeth Dole's understanding of homelessness? Discuss and share. What words would you and your study group use to describe Homeless-1's experience of homelessness? Discuss and share. What words would you and your study group use to describe Homeless-2's experience of homelessness? Discuss and share. What words would you and your study group use to describe Homeless-3's experience of homelessness. Discuss and share. What words would you and your study group use to describe the Director and Host's reaction to the homeless? Discuss and share.

In Scene Three, what does Homeless-4 ask of us? What does Homeless-5 ask of us? What does Homeless-6 ask of us? Discuss and share. I would like you and your study group to consider what prayers you would compose and pray on behalf of the homeless.

5. I invite you and your study group to explore some of the cinematic, literary and institutional resources that will help shed light on homelessness in our society. *With Honors* is a film that demonstrates how a young college student's attitude toward the homeless changes as he develops a relationship with a homeless person.

Another fine film that deals with homelessness in our society in a very sobering manner is a film made for television which aired on ABC. It is entitled *God Bless the Child* and stars Mare Winningham.

There are a number of books that explore the history, the causes and the dilemma of homelessness in our society. Two of note are *Rachel's*

Children by Jonathan Koziol (New York: Fawcett Columbine, 1988) and *Street Journal: Finding God in the Homeless* by Gary N. Smith, S.J. (Kansas City, MO: Sheed & Ward, 1994).

Why not explore what institutional services and resources you have in your local community to meet the needs of the homeless. I suggest you contact the local Council of Churches to see if they have any resources. Also contact both your city and state Social Service offices and explore what institutional resources are available for the homeless in your community. If you can't find any, keep looking and continue raising the question about why there aren't any or more resources to meet the needs of these "voiceless" and "powerless" members of the community.

6. Carroll Stuhlmueller, C.P., in his commentary on "Deutero-Isaiah and Trito-Isaiah" (*New Jerome Biblical Commentary,* p. 345), points out that "fasting enables comfortable people to share the lot of the hungry poor and from this hunger to look to God as the source of life and nourishment. To fast and yet neglect the poor perverts religion." Here I propose an exercise to help you and your study group to *experientially* understand and appreciate what it means to be homeless. Do one of the following: (a) Contact the Department of Social Services and find out about the qualifications for assistance. (b) Find out where you could stay if you needed emergency shelter tonight. Perhaps you'll visit that place and speak to a resident or a manager. (c) Visit the housing authority and find out how you would get a subsidized apartment. (d) Visit the food stamp office and find out if you qualify. Apply for aid. (e) Visit a soup kitchen, shelter or other service-providing agency and find out what they are all about. These ideas were suggested by Henry Ostendorf. They come from the syllabus he created for a course he taught at San Francisco State University entitled "Out of Control: The Homeless Experience."

Once you and your study group have exercised one or more of these experiential options, get together to discuss and share what you thought, felt, sensed, experienced and learned about being homeless from these experiences.

7. John Vanier, the founder of the L'Arche communities, has helped us realize that in community we not only minister to others in their obvious needs but that they minister to us in our less obvious needs. How can you and your study group minister to the poor in your city? What can the

poor teach you about God and life? Discuss and share. How can you and your study group minister to the hungry in your city? What can the hungry teach you about God and life? Discuss and share. How can you and your study group minister to the homeless in your city? What can the homeless teach you about God and life? Discuss and share.

8. I invite you and your study group to explore the following questions. Who are the *voiceless* in your Church, your school, your city, your state/province, your country and throughout the world? Discuss and share. What are some practical and concrete ways that you and your study group can become "voices for the voiceless" in society today? Discuss and share.

Who are the *powerless* in your Church, your school, your city, your state/province, your country and throughout the world? Discuss and share. What are some practical and concrete ways that you and your study group can become "power for the powerless" in society today? Discuss and share.

Now I invite you and your study group to conclude this exercise by composing a cinquain on three subjects: (1) The Voiceless; (2) The Powerless; (3) The Homeless. If you are not familiar with the literary form of the cinquain, refer to reflection question 8 from the biblical drama *What Happens Next?* What do your *cinquains* reveal that you and your study group have learned about the voiceless, the powerless, and the homeless? Discuss and share.

9. Last Supper Discourse

(John 14:1-12)

"Let not your hearts be troubled; believe in God, believe also in me. In my Father's house are many rooms; if it were not so, would I have told you that I go to prepare a place for you? And when I go and prepare a place for you, I will come again and will take you to myself, that where I am you may be also. And you know the way where I am going." Thomas said to him, "Lord, we do not know where you are going; how can we know the way?" Jesus said to him, "I am the way, and the truth, and the life; no one comes to the Father, but by me. If you had known me, you would have known my Father also; henceforth you know him and have seen him." Philip said to him, "Lord, show us the Father, and we shall be satisfied." Jesus said to him, "Have I been with you so long, and yet you do not know me, Philip? He who has seen me has seen the Father; how can you say, 'Show us the Father'? Do you not believe that I am in the Father and the Father in me? The words that I say to you I do not speak on my own authority; but the Father who dwells in me does his works. Believe me that I am in the Father and Father in me; or else believe me for the sake of the works themselves. Truly, truly, I say to you, he who believes in me will also do the works that I do; and greater works than these will he do, because I go to the Father."

Many Places in a Mother's Heart

CAST

Crutches-1 (Mark)   Worker (Aimee)
Crutches-2 (Linda)   Manager (Ed)
Friend-1   Mother
Friend-2   Student-1
Friend-3   Student-2
Friend-4 (Kristie)   Mourner
Volunteer (Christi)   Cook

SCENE ONE

CRUTCHES-1:

[C-1 comes into the acting area on crutches. He reaches the center and stops there, sore and exhausted, in order to rest and catch his breath.] I hate these damn things! I have finally found something I'm good at. Just call me "King Klutz!" [Friend-1 and Friend-2 come in absorbed in conversation. They do not notice C-1.]

FRIEND-1:

But the amazing thing is I have heard the story of the Good Samaritan a thousand times and never made the connection.

FRIEND-2:

What connection?

FRIEND-1:

That it's a story about compassion.

FRIEND-2:

So, what's the big deal?

FRIEND-1:

Compassion, you idiot! The word literally means "to cry out with." So the story challenges us to identify with and feel the pain and the joy of others.

FRIEND-2:

Say, wasn't that Mark Lang we just passed on crutches?

FRIEND-1:

It couldn't be. Mark Lang doesn't wear crutches. [They continue off into the congregation and freeze.]

CRUTCHES-1:

[Mark takes a few steps and then Friend-3, who is obviously in a hurry, comes rushing in.]

FRIEND-3:

Oh my God! Is this a vision I see before my eyes? Mark Lang, how are you?

CRUTCHES-1:

Well, to be perfectly honest....[Friend-3 cuts him off.]

FRIEND-3:

No, don't tell me! Let me look at you. [She looks at him.] Did you have your hair cut?

CRUTCHES-1:

No.

FRIEND-3:

Have you lost weight?

CRUTCHES-1:

No. Why do you ask?

FRIEND-3:

I don't know. There's just something different about you and I can't figure out what it is.

CRUTCHES-1:

Maybe it's the crutches.

FRIEND-3:

See, I knew there was something. Well, Mark, it's been great talking with you. Oh my God, look at the time. I'm late for class. Gotta run. Good seeing you, Mark.

CRUTCHES-1:

Yeah. Good seeing you. [Friend-3 runs off into the congregation and freezes.] Well, maybe I'll drag myself over to the Mission Gardens. [He moves a bit and Friend-4 starts jumping up and down trying to dislodge something from an imaginary bush or tree.] Hi, Kristie.

FRIEND-4:

Oh, hi, Mark. [Friend-4 continues to try and dislodge whatever is stuck.]

CRUTCHES-1:

What are you doing, Kristie?

FRIEND-4:

My frisbee sailed up into this tree and now it's stuck. I'm just not tall enough. If I could find a stick or something I know I could get it down. Hey, I'll bet this crutch would work. [She grabs one of Mark's crutches and begins using it to dislodge her imaginary frisbee. Mark falls down as soon as Kristie grabs the crutch.] Ha! There it is. Guess this was my lucky day. I never dreamt I would run into someone on crutches today. Thanks, Mark. [She throws the crutch back to him.] See you around! [Friend-4 takes off, throwing the frisbee into the congregation. She freezes.]

CRUTCHES-1:

[Crutches-1 gradually picks himself up and brushes himself off. Crutches-2 comes in and meets him.] Linda, it looks as though you got hit by the same train I did. Are you all right?

183

CRUTCHES-2:

I'll live… barely!

CRUTCHES-1:

What happened?

CRUTCHES-2:

I was playing volleyball over by the Grahams and twisted my ankle on a hidden sprinkler head.

CRUTCHES-1:

Is it going to be O.K.?

CRUTCHES-2:

[Crutches-2 is constantly moving on.] The doctor said he has to wait until the swelling goes down before he can tell if I need surgery. God, I hope I don't. That's all I need to complicate my life. I can see myself at graduation crawling up the platform to get my diploma.

CRUTCHES-1:

I know what you mean. The doctor says I'm going to have to have surgery.

CRUTCHES-2:

That's nice. Well, Mark, I'd love to stay and chat but I've got to get over to the Info Booth to try to get tickets to the Senior Booze Cruise. Nice talking to you. Later.

CRUTCHES-1:

[Discouraged.] Yeah, later. [Crutches-1 wanders back upstage to a bench where there is a phone. He sits down, puts his crutches down, picks up the phone and dials a number.] Hi, Mom, guess who? Well, not so good. What's the matter? Where do I begin? [Crutches-1 freezes for a few moments and then all of the players in Scene One move off to be replaced by the players in Scene Two.]

SCENE TWO

[This scene is set with four different vignettes coming alive at different times. They are spokes of a wheel. A Mother-figure is at the hub. She moves toward a character in each scene that comes alive. She also gives different characters a symbolic object that will be used to set the eucharistic table at the end of this scene. Those objects are two candles, bread, and a carafe of wine.]

WORKER:

[She knocks on the door.]

MANAGER:

The door's open. Come on in. [He looks up and sees Worker.] Hi, Aimee. What's up?

WORKER:

I've come to tell you that I am going to take a leave of absence.

MANAGER:

You're kidding. What on earth for?

WORKER:

My husband and I have decided to have a baby.

MANAGER:

Are you out of your mind, Aimee? This could really jeopardize your career. You stay out of the computer graphics field for a year or two and you're through. Be reasonable, Aimee. Don't throw a promising career away.

WORKER:

This may not make sense to you, Ed, but I remember something my mother always quoted from the author of *The Little Prince.*

MOTHER:

"It is only with the heart that one can see rightly; what is essential is invisible to the eye." [Mother puts carafe of wine on a bar stool near the Worker.]

WORKER:

Let's just say I have to follow my heart. [Both Manager and Worker freeze.]

MOURNER:

[The Mourner is kneeling down and praying in church.] I guess I may be an infrequent visitor at your house. I seem to forget you when things are going well for me and I'm always asking for help when things are going bad. But I haven't got anyplace else to go. I'm hurt. I'm angry. I'm lost and confused. I found it hard when my mother died two years ago. But now my niece is very sick. The doctors at Stanford are not sure they can save her. I'm not even sure what it is I want to ask. But help me. Please, help me.

MOTHER:

[Mother brings a lit candle and puts it on a bar stool next to the Mourner.] Remember the prayer I used to pray when I felt helpless and confused? "God, grant me the serenity to accept the things I cannot change, the courage to change the things I can, and the wisdom to know the difference." [Mourner freezes and Mother moves back up to the center of the stage area.]

STUDENT-1:

But you always struck me as a pretty laid-back character. Then you start going to Monday evening Social Justice Study groups. Why should you be concerned about what happens to blacks in South Africa? What difference does it make to you what women, gays and people of color on this campus are protesting about?

STUDENT-2:

First off, I am as confused as you are about a lot of what is happening on this campus and in the world. But one night I was thinking about all of this and I remembered a story my Mom had told me.

MOTHER:

[Brings a lit candle down to the bar stool near Student-2 and leaves it there.] So the Teacher asked her students: "How do you know that night has ended and day is on the way back?" One student said: "Is it when you look at the horizon and can tell the difference between an oak tree and a pine tree?" The Teacher said: "No." Another student spoke up: "Is it when you look in the distance and can tell whether the animal you see is a bear or a wolf?" "No," said the Teacher. "When is it, then?" the students asked. "It's when you look into the face of the person next to you and can

186

see in that face your brother or your sister. Because until you can do that, no matter what time it is, it is still night."

STUDENT-2:

You see, the way I look at it, wherever there's discrimination in any of the thousand disguises it comes in, it's still night.

STUDENT-1:

So? Are you going to save the world, Mark?

STUDENT-2:

No. But I think each of us has some light within us. There's too much darkness for one person but I can bring a little more light right here where I stand and work and live. My Mom taught me that light has many different names. One of those names is love. [Student-1 and Student-2 freeze as Mother moves back to the center stage area.]

VOLUNTEER:

Do you mind if I ask you a personal question?

COOK:

As long as it's not how old I am.

VOLUNTEER:

I would never dream of being so indelicate.

COOK:

Go ahead, Christi, ask away.

VOLUNTEER:

Well, I've been coming here to the Julian Street Inn for almost nine months. You could cook anywhere. Why did you choose to work here?

COOK:

First, Christi, tell me why you've been coming down here to help all year?

VOLUNTEER:

Lots of reasons.

COOK:

Like?

VOLUNTEER:

Like life is too comfortable back at school. Like it's easy to forget there actually are people who are poor or hungry or homeless when you live where I live and as I live. Like I want to love others but I don't think I can do that until I know what brings them pain. Like I'm no Mother Teresa but I remember something she said:

MOTHER:

"What I'm doing may only be a drop of water to quench enormous thirst. But without my small drop that thirst would be much greater."

VOLUNTEER:

So what I do may be a small drop, but it's all I have to give. And I want to give it.

COOK:

Where I grew up, my father had a bakery in an older, poorer part of town. It broke my heart seeing all those hungry people with no place to go and no future because we all tried to make them invisible. I remember telling my Mother how sad and frustrated I was that I couldn't help them. She said:

MOTHER:

"Who says you can't?" [Mother brings bread and puts it on the bar stool near the Cook.]

COOK:

I said to her: "But Mom, the only things I know how to do well are bake and cook. What good will that do them?" She just said:

MOTHER:

"You can only give them what you have to give them."

COOK:

Not feeling up to the enormity of the need, I reluctantly confessed to her: "Maybe someday, Mom, somewhere, someone will do something about it." She looked me straight in the eyes. This body language always alerted me that she was about to present me with a major piece of truth that I probably wouldn't want to hear. Then she said something that changed my life.

MOTHER:

"If not you, then who? If not now, then when? If not here, then where?"

COOK:

So, Christi, here I am twenty years later doing what I do best and giving the only gift I know how to give. Like you, I think it's only a drop. Maybe someday all those drops will add up to something. [Volunteer and Cook freeze.]

MOTHER:

[Mother beckons all the characters to come up to her on the main stage acting area. As all the characters slowly turn and come up toward her, two people carry the altar table into a central place. All the characters place their respective symbolic objects on the altar. They join hands and together pray:]

ALL:

We give you thanks, compassionate God, for these and all your gifts which we have received because you love us through Christ our Lord. [All the characters freeze as a recording of "Another Day in Paradise" by Phil Collins comes on. After a minute or so, the characters return to their places in the congregation. The music continues for another minute or two and then fades out.]

—FINIS—

PROPS

1. Two (2) Sets of Crutches.
2. One (1) Telephone.
3. Four (4) Bar Stools or their equivalent that act as stands for the Telephone in Scene One and the two Candles, Bread and Carafe of Wine in Scene Two.
4. Two (2) Candles in Holders.
5. One (1) Loaf of Bread.

6. One (1) Carafe of Wine.
7. One (1) Recording (cassette tape or compact disc) of Phil Collins' song "Another Day in Paradise."

PRODUCTION NOTES

This biblical drama was designed and performed as part of a liturgy on the fifth Sunday of Easter, in Year "A." The two scripture readings that the biblical drama interprets are Acts 6:1-7 and John 14:1-12. The Biblical Explorers attempted to make some "connections" between the realities of the early Church and the realities of their life, between the challenges of the early Church and the challenges they were facing at this time in their life.

Something else that influenced the final shape of this drama was the fact that this Sunday in May also happened to be Mother's Day in the United States. The role of the mother as the one you can count on to listen to you (Scene One) and as the embodiment of compassion and wisdom (Scene Two) found confirming parallels in some of the scriptural images of God as a loving Mother as well as the testimony of the Biblical Explorers from their own personal experience of the presence of loving mothers in their lives.

In the second scene, the Mother places one of the four Eucharistic symbols (i.e. a lit candle on two different occasions, the loaf of bread and the carafe of wine) on a bar stool next to a character. These symbols are taken by the characters and placed on the altar at the end of the biblical drama. In this way, the biblical dramatization culminates in the preparation of the gifts. Feel free to adapt this aspect of the drama. In many parishes the gifts are brought up by representatives of the congregation after the collection has been taken up. If you prefer to do it this way, simply adjust the conclusion of the biblical drama.

The song by Phil Collins entitled "Another Day in Paradise" was suggested by one of the Biblical Explorers. One of the members of your study group may have a suggestion for a liturgical or contemporary song that would serve as a better reflection on the scriptures that were just heard and the biblical drama that was just seen. Incorporate the suggestions and adaptations of your study group wherever possible. It is through such suggestions and adaptations that the members of your study group make these biblical dramas their own.

In Scene Two, Student-1 refers to the Monday evening Social Justice Study groups. These were sponsored and organized by Campus Ministry at Santa Clara University. The student and staff coordinators would try to get members of the faculty and outside guests to speak on contemporary issues as well as national and international concerns that brought together the concerns of "religious faith" and "action for justice." While they may not be called by the same name, schools and parishes have many such presentations throughout the year. This is another place where it would be good to adapt the script to meet the experiences and needs of the faith community with which you are working.

REFLECTION QUESTIONS AND EXERCISES

1. How would you and your study group describe the differences between "old-timers" and "newcomers"? Imagine what some of the attitudes and behaviors of the "old-timers" toward the "newcomers" might be. Are these attitudes and behaviors just? Do the Gospels offer you any suggestions about what are appropriate attitudes and behaviors toward "newcomers"? Describe and share.

How would you and your study group describe the differences between "insiders" and "outsiders"? Imagine what some of the attitudes and behaviors of "insiders" toward "outsiders" might be. Are these attitudes and behaviors just? Do the Gospels offer you any suggestions about what are appropriate attitudes and behaviors toward "outsiders"? Discuss and share.

In the scripture passage from the Acts of the Apostles, the Greek disciples are complaining. What does the title "disciple" mean? If disciple comes from a Latin word meaning "learner," what are these disciples learning? Who is their teacher? Discuss and share.

The Greek disciples are complaining that their widows are being neglected. What do the widows symbolize and represent in the society of the early Church? What would be a modern-day equivalent of "widows" today? Discuss and share. I would like you and your study group to consider the ways that you consciously and unconsciously ignore the needs of contemporary outsiders. Discuss and share.

2. I invite you and your study group to consider a passage from James 2:17-17. What do you and your study group think the writer means when he says that "faith by itself, if it has no works, is dead"? Do you

and your study group agree or disagree with this assessment? Discuss and share.

I would like you and your study group to consider the following question. What are some of your religious values? Discuss and share these values. In a sense, these values constitute a creed of what you believe in. Compose a creed that everyone in your group can affirm. Compare and contrast what you and your study group believe with "Credo" by Michael E. Moynahan, S.J. in *God of Seasons* (San Jose, CA: Resource Publications, 1980, pp. 11-13) as well as the Masai Creed and the Creed of Young People from Berard Marthaller's *The Creed: The Apostolic Faith In Contemporary Theology* (Mystic, Connecticut: Twenty-Third Publications, 1993). Discuss and share. Do you and your study group think that your actions for justice reveal what you value or believe? Why or why not? Discuss and share.

What is a hypocrite? What do you and your study group think of people who say one thing and do another? What do you and your study group think a religious hypocrite would be? How easy or hard is it to let the Gospel values influence and shape our attitudes and behavior toward widows, toward the poor, toward the voiceless and the powerless, toward the marginated in our community and our society? Discuss and share.

What do you and your study group think is the relationship between "faith" and "action for justice"? Is this ultimately what the author of the letter of James is describing? Discuss and share.

3. In the passage from St. John's Gospel, the term "the way" appears three times. Jesus says to the disciples: "You know *the way* that leads where I go." Thomas replies: "Lord, we do not know where you are going. How can we know *the way?*" Then Jesus says: "I am *the way,* and the truth, and the life; no one comes to the Father but through me."

Throughout the Gospels and the Acts of the Apostles, the term "the way" refers to the followers of Jesus. See Mk 10:52, Lk 17:11, Lk 20:21, Jn 14:16, Acts 9:2, Acts 16:17, and Acts 19:23. "The way" is used in these texts and others as well. I invite you and your study group to become good detectives. Take one of the synoptic Gospels and study it together. What clues and evidence can you discover from what Jesus says and what Jesus does that you might piece together as "the way" that all who call themselves his disciples are to follow? Discuss and share.

Where did Jesus' journey lead him? What does Jerusalem symbolize or represent in the life of the disciple and the Church? What does it represent in your own faith journey? Did the disciples understand or willingly embrace the suffering and death about which Jesus spoke to them? What is the paschal mystery? How is the paschal mystery celebrated in every Eucharistic liturgy? How is the paschal mystery at the heart of what it means to be a disciple of Jesus? Can one truly follow Christ on "the way" and escape the suffering, dying and rising that he experienced? Why or why not? Discuss and share.

What do you and your study group think Jesus means when he says "I am *the way*"? What evidence can you and your study group provide from the Gospels that demonstrate that Jesus' claim that he is "the way" is valid? Discuss and share. What do you and your study group think Jesus means when he says "I am *the truth*"? What evidence can you and your study group provide from the Gospels that Jesus' claim that he is "the truth" is valid? Discuss and share. What do you and your study group think Jesus means when he says "I am *the life*"? What evidence can you and your study group provide from the Gospels that demonstrates that Jesus' claim that he is "the life" is valid? Discuss and share.

4. In Scene One, how do the different characters respond to Crutches-1? What are the two friends discussing who don't even see Crutches-1? In the scriptural story that Friend-1 and Friend-2 are discussing, do any characters fail to see a person in need? What do you and your study group think prevents us from seeing people in need around us? What do you and your study group think prevents us from responding to those people in need around us? What steps do you think you can take to see and respond to more of the people in need around you? Discuss and share.

What is Friend-3's response to Crutches-1? What prevents this character from seeing and responding to Crutches-1? How do you and your study group think the "pace of your life" affects what you see and don't see? How do you and your study group think the "pace of your life" affects how you do and don't respond to those in need around you? What practical and concrete steps can you and your study group take in order to change the pace of your life and see more of the people in need around you? Discuss and share.

How does Friend-4 respond to Crutches-1? Do you and your study group think you can sometimes be so focused on your own needs that you are blinded to the needs of others? Can you and your study group think of any ways to prevent your own needs from blinding you to the needs of others around you? Discuss and share.

How does Crutches-2 respond to Crutches-1? How do you and your study group imagine that Crutches-1's Mother responds to his predicament? Which of the characters in Scene One did you expect to respond to Crutches-1? Which of the characters in Scene One actually responded to the needs of Crutches-1? Why was this character able to respond when the other characters in the scene were not? Discuss and share.

5. Scene Two consists of four vignettes. What do you and your study group think is the reason for the Worker's decision to take a "leave of absence"? How does the Manager respond to her decision to take this "leave of absence"? Where does the Worker find the *wisdom* and the *strength* to make this change in her career? What do you and your study group think the following quote from *The Little Prince* means? "It is only with the heart that one can see rightly; what is essential is invisible to the eye." Discuss and share. What gift does the mother give to the Worker? What do you and your study group think the wine represents? Discuss and share.

In the second vignette of Scene Two, a Mourner is praying in church. What do you and your study group think the Mourner is praying about? Why is the Mourner hurt, angry, lost and confused? If you have/had experienced the death of a loved one, would you experience some of this same hurt, anger, and confusion? Discuss and share. The Mourner tells God that "I'm not even sure what it is I want to ask." If you were in the Mourner's situation, what would you ask for? If you know of anyone who has recently lost a parent, a sibling, a relative or friend through death, what can you and your study group ask God for him/her?

I invite you and your study group to reflect on Romans 8:26-27. What do you and your study group think St. Paul means when he says "the Spirit helps us in our weakness"? Discuss and share. What do you and your study group think St. Paul means when he says that "the Spirit intercedes with sighs too deep for words"? Discuss and share. What do you and your study group think St. Paul means when he says that "the Spirit intercedes for the saints, according to the will of God"? Discuss and share. What do you and your study group think is the significance of the lighted candle that the Mother places on the stool next to the Mourner? Discuss and share. I encourage you and your study group to conclude this part of your reflective discussion with a prayer of St. Paul's found in Ephesians 3:14-21.

194

What do you and your study group think Student-2 is concerned about in the third vignette from Scene Two? Discuss and share. How do you and your study group respond to the story that the Mother tells about how you know when night has ended and day is on the way back? Discuss and share. Student-2 says that her mother taught her that "light has many different names." What do you and your study group think some of those names of light might be? Discuss and share. The Mother brings a lit candle and places it on a stool next to Student-2. What do you and your study group think this represents? Discuss and share.

In the fourth vignette from Scene Two, what are the reasons that the Volunteer gives for working in a homeless shelter? There is a story of a rabbi that states: "To love, to really love, means to know what brings your neighbor pain." Would you and your study group agree or disagree with the rabbi's explanation of love? Discuss and share. The Mother brings a loaf of bread and places it on a stool next to the Cook. What do you and your study group think this bread represents? Discuss and share.

6. In Scene Two, the Mother brings a lit candle to the Mourner and reminds him of the Serenity Prayer that she taught him. What do you and your study group think are some of the things in your school, your Church, your city, your state/province, your country and world that need to be changed? What does it mean to pray: "God, grant me the strength to change the things I can"? Why does change, real change, require strength? Discuss and share.

What do you and your study group think are some of the things in your school, your Church, your city, your state/province, your country and world that cannot be changed? Why can't these things be changed? What does it mean to pray: "God, grant me the courage to accept the things I cannot change"? Why does acceptance of things we cannot change require courage? Discuss and share.

What do you and your study group think is the reason for praying: "God, give us the wisdom to know the difference"? What do you and your study group think "wisdom" means? Why is wisdom necessary to know the difference between the things we can change and those we can't? Where would you and your study group look for such wisdom? Discuss and share. Do the gifts that the Mother gives to different people in Scene Two give you and your study group any clues about some traditional sources of wisdom in the Church? How can you and your study group discover the wisdom you need (i.e. to discern the difference between what you can and cannot change) in the scriptures? Discuss and share. How can you and your study group discover the wisdom you need in the sacramental life of the Church? Discuss and share. How can you and your study group discover the wisdom you need in the lives of those holy men and women who have gone before you in faith? Discuss and share. It might be helpful to focus on the particular life of a saint whose life and example offers you such wisdom. How do you and your study group discover the wisdom you need in the life of the faith community? Discuss and share.

7. What do you and your study group think are some of the more blatant forms of discrimination in your community, your Church and society today? Discuss and share. What do you and your study group think are some of the more subtle forms of discrimination in your community, your Church and society today? Discuss and share.

Do you and your study group agree or disagree with the statement of Student-2 that wherever there's discrimination in any of the thousand guises it comes in, "it is still night"? Discuss and share. How is discrimination expressed in attitudes? How is discrimination expressed in behaviors? What's one form of discrimination you and your study group can identify in your Church, your school, your city, your state/province, your country and the world? What are some concrete actions that you and your study group can take to put an end to this particular manifestation of "night"? Discuss and share and then take some positive and constructive action.

8. Scene Two ends with all of the characters praying a prayer of gratitude for the blessings and gifts that God has given them. Celtic Spirituality has a wonderful sense of thanksgiving expressed in its prayers and poems. One example from the *Carmina Gadelica,* edited by Alexander Carmichael, illustrates this beautifully.

> Each thing I have received from Thee it came,
> Each thing for which I hope, from Thy love it will come,
> Each thing I enjoy, it is of Thy bounty,
> Each thing I ask, comes of Thy disposing.
> (Quoted in *The Celtic Way of Prayer* by Esther De Waal, London: Hodder and Stoughton, 1996, p. 178.)

I invite you and your study group to consider the blessings and gifts that God has given you and to offer a prayer of thanks. You might invite people to jot down on a piece of paper the things that come to mind for them as you lead them in this exercise of "remembering and giving thanks." When the members of your study group share the gifts and blessings they have received, this will suggest additional blessings to the other members of your group.

First, consider the gifts and blessings that you and your study group have experienced in nature. Do you experience creation as a gift? Do you experience God's blessing in the seas and dry land? Do you experience God's blessing in the different seasons of the year? Do you experience God's blessing when you see flowers or trees in bloom? Do you experience God's blessing when you see creatures that crawl and creatures that swim?

Second, consider the gifts and blessings you and your study group have received in your personal genealogy. Do you experience your ethnic and cultural origins as a blessing from God? Do you experience your parents as a blessing from God? Do you experience your brothers and sisters as a blessing from God? Do you experience your aunts and uncles, your cousins and relatives as blessings or gifts from God? Do you consider any teachers, colleagues or friends as blessings from God? How do these people reveal the presence and love of God to you? Is this something for which you can give thanks?

Third, consider the mystery of your own creation. Do you experience your life as a blessing or gift from God? How do you discover the presence and love of God through your five senses? Do you experience your seeing, hearing, smelling, tasting and touching as blessings from God? Do you experience your thinking and feeling and sensing as gifts from God? Do you experience the presence and love of God in your talents and abilities? Do you experience your attitudes and behaviors as blessings from God?

Fourth, consider the needs of the voiceless, the powerless and the marginated of society. Can you give thanks to God for the blessing of the poor? What do the poor teach us about the presence and love of God? How does the way we respond to the poor around us reveal to them the presence and love of God? Can you and your study group give thanks for the presence of Christ you encounter in them and the compassion of Christ that they experience in your response to their needs? Can you give thanks to God for the blessing of the voiceless and powerless? What do the voiceless and powerless teach us about the presence and love of God? How does the way we respond to the voiceless and powerless around us reveal to them the presence and love of God? Can you and your study group give thanks for the presence of Christ that you encounter in them and the compassion of Christ that they can experience in your Christian response to their needs?

When you and your study group have jotted down a number of the blessings you have received, proceed to do a litany of thanks. Have someone announce: "Let us remember and give thanks to God for the blessings of creation." Then have the participants mention one of the blessings that they remembered in this area: "For the gift of...(fill in the blank)" and have everyone in the group respond: "We give you thanks, O Lord." After you have gone through all four categories, you might conclude with the Lord's Prayer or a doxology: "Glory be to the Father and to the Son and to the Holy Spirit, as it was in the beginning, is now, and ever shall be, world without end. Amen."